A Guide to Special Collections in the OCLC Database

Compiled and edited by
Philip Schieber
Virginia G. Voedisch
Becky A. Wright

Designed by
Rick Limes
Karen Dodson

OCLC Online Computer Library Center, Inc.
6565 Frantz Road
Dublin, Ohio 43017-0702
(614) 764-6000

A special note of thanks to the libraries that contributed illustrations and information about their collections.

Contents

A Guide to the Database

A Canoe of the Friendly Islands
Published Dec' 24 1782 by G. Robinson

Canoe of the Friendly Islands. From An Authentic Narrative of a Voyage Performed by Captain Cook and Captain Clerke in His Majesty's Ships Resolution and Discovery, *by William Ellis, assistant surgeon to both vessels. William F. Charters South Seas Collection, Butler University.*

elcome to the riches of the OCLC database—4,138 years of information.

Through OCLC, libraries have merged their catalogs electronically, making available to libraries and, ultimately, to their patrons, resources that no single institution could possess. The OCLC database contains over 20 million bibliographic records spanning four millenia of recorded knowledge, from approximately 2150 B.C. to the present. The oldest item identified in the database is a terra cotta cone with a Babylonian inscription, cataloged by Dartmouth University (OCLC #3244509).

This unique store of knowledge encompasses records in eight formats—books, serials, sound recordings, musical scores, audiovisual media, maps, archives and manuscripts, and machine-readable data files.

Like the knowledge it records, the database grows steadily. More than 23,000 records are added each week by OCLC member libraries.

Through a network of more than 200,000 miles of telecommunications lines, OCLC makes this store of information available to libraries and their users.

Libraries use information in the OCLC database to:

- Acquire and catalog books and other materials
- Order custom-printed catalog cards and/or machine-readable records for local catalogs
- Maintain information on journals and periodicals
- Arrange interlibrary loans
- Maintain location information on library materials

Library patrons use information in the OCLC database to:

- Conduct research
- Compile bibliographies
- Verify citations
- Gather information for subsequent searching in other sources
- Find the location of specific items
- Find the works of a specific author

Title page of Loci Communes, *from the collection of Bethany Lutheran Theological Seminary.*

An International, Multilingual Compilation

Created, assembled, and nurtured by libraries for libraries and their patrons, the OCLC database reaches more than 8,000 libraries of all types in 26 countries, including: Australia, Barbados, Belgium, Canada, People's Republic of China, Costa Rica, Denmark, Federal Republic of Germany, Finland, France, Iceland, Ireland, Italy, Japan, Mexico, The Netherlands, Oman, Puerto Rico, Saudi Arabia, Spain, Sweden, Switzerland, Taiwan, United Kingdom, United States, and Vatican City.

Reflecting this broadening base of contributors, an increasingly large percentage of records in the database represents items published in languages other than English, French, Spanish, or German, in alphabets from Arabic to Nahuatl (a chiefly pictographic language). For a list of languages represented in the database, see Appendix A.

Programs

This internationalization has been paralleled by programs specifically intended to enrich the database. Retrospective conversion projects have added more than 10 million records to the database, many of them from geographic and subject-oriented special collections.

In 1986, for example, the U.S. Department of Education funded 19 project grants, totaling $3.14 million, involving the OCLC database. See Appendix B for a list of these projects.

The CONSER (Cooperative Online Serials) Program involves 20 major university libraries which add, authenticate, and upgrade serials (journals) cataloging information in the database and provide ongoing maintenance for serials catalog records.

```
   Screen 1 of 2
▶NO HOLDINGS IN OCL - FOR HOLDINGS ENTER dh DEPRESS DISPLAY RECD SEND
   OCLC: 13555900      Rec stat: c Entrd: 880512        Used: 880528
▶Type: a Bib lvl: m Govt pub:        Lang: jpn Source: d Illus:
   Repr:   Enc lvl: I Conf pub: 0 Ctrl: ja Dat tp: s M/F/B: 10
   Indx: 0 Mod rec: r Festschr: 0 Cont:
   Desc: a Int lvl:    Dates: 1977,
   ▶ 1 010
   ▶ 2 040       IUL ‡c IUL
   ▶ 3 020       4007300014
   ▶ 4 090       BL2222.T445 ‡b F85 1977
   ▶ 5 090       ‡b
   ▶ 6 049       OCLC
   ▶ 7 100 10    Fukaya, Tadamasa, ‡d 1012-
   ▶ 8 100 10    浮谷忠政, ‡d 1012-
   ▶ 9 245 10    Tenriku-o ku-ogigaku josetsu / ‡c Fukaya Tadamasa.

   Screen 2 of 2
  ▶10 245 10    天理教教義学序説 / ‡c 浮谷忠
政 .
  ▶11 250       Shohan.
  ▶12 250       初版 .
  ▶13 260 0     Tenri-shi : ‡b Tenriku-o D-ou-usha, ‡c Sh-owa 52
  (1977) ‡g (1983 printing)
  ▶14 260 0     天理市 : ‡b 天理教道友社,
  ‡c 昭和52 (1977) ‡g (1983 printing)
  ▶15 300       337 p. : ‡c 21 cm.
  ▶16 610 20    Tenriku-o ‡x Doctrines.
  ▶17 610 20    天理教 ‡x Doctrines.
```

The OCLC database contains the world's largest assemblage of bibliographic records in vernacular Chinese, Japanese, and Korean. More than 80,000 records are available. This record provides information in both the roman alphabet and Chinese character sets.

8

The U.S. Newspaper Program will eventually encompass more than 300,000 newspaper titles published in North America since 1690, providing not only bibliographic and location information, but also for preservation of important and endangered collections. Under the auspices of the National Endowment for the Humanities, newspaper repository libraries are contributing cataloging information to the database—detailed descriptions about what volumes and issues of a particular newspaper a library holds. Researchers, writers, historians, and scholars can now go to one source to find a newspaper and its closest location, whether a contemporary daily or such early Kansas papers as *The Cain City Razzooper, The Astonisher and Paralyzer, Yellow Dog,* and *Unmuzzled Truth.*

The Major Microforms project increases access to yet another special subset of materials. For example, the University of Utah Libraries undertook a two-year project to catalog and enter into the OCLC database the more than 9,000 titles in the Landmarks of Science microfilm set published by the Readex Microprint Corporation. The set encompasses scientific monographs dating from the beginning of printing (1450). A list of other microform sets whose cataloging is either in progress or completed appears in Appendix C.

Drawing of a colonial wooden hand press.

Cataloging Formats

The OCLC Online System uses eight cataloging formats derived from the Library of Congress **MA**chine-**R**eadable **C**ataloging (MARC) formats for communication of bibliographic information in machine-readable form. Bibliographic records entered into the database must conform to one of these formats, but each one has a great degree of flexibility, as can be seen from the variety of materials they encompass. New methods of recording and transferring the accumulated knowledge of mankind—machine-readable data files and electronic document delivery—are ready and waiting to be implemented.

Each institution participating in the OCLC Cataloging Subsystem contributes bibliographic records; OCLC users contribute over 68% of the more than 18 million bibliographic records in the Online Union Catalog. (A thorough description of the Online Union Catalog appears in Appendix D.) The remaining records are contributed by the Library of Congress, the British Library, the National Library of Canada, the National Agricultural Library, and the National Library of Medicine (CATLINE records). The special collections described in this publication constitute a fraction of this wealth of knowledge.

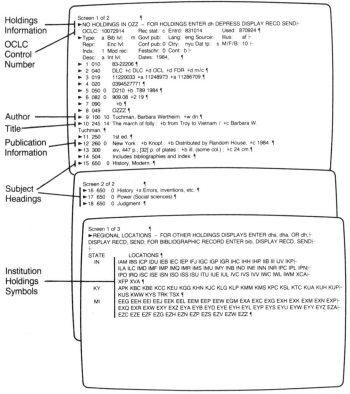

*A typical MARC (**MA**chine-**R**eadable **C**ataloging) record contains a physical description of an item and information about its intellectual content. Also attached to each record in the OCLC database is a list of member libraries that hold the item. Each library has a unique three-character institution holdings symbol, and the symbols are arranged alphabetically by state or country.*

Books

By far, the largest percentage of records in the database (85.18%) is in the books format. Books are defined as separately published, monographic printed items (books, pamphlets, textual sheets and broadsides, sets of activity cards, etc.), published atlases, theses and dissertations (originals and reproductions or copies), original monographic microform publications, and individual technical reports. This broad category covers such diverse items as stamp or coin catalogs; legislation, legal cases, and case notes; and abstracts/summaries and book reviews.

The 1855 edition of Walt Whitman's Leaves of Grass *was the millionth volume acquired by the Kent State University Library (in 1974). It is part of an extensive American poetry collection.*

Serials

A serial is a publication in any medium, issued in successive parts bearing numerical or chronological designations, and intended to be continued indefinitely. In libraries oriented toward current research, contemporary developments, or archival studies of what were once contemporary matters, serials may be the most heavily used items in the collection.

The serials format (5.89% of the database) covers textual serial publications (print or microform) and reproductions of such publications. This definition includes magazines; newspapers; annual reports, yearbooks, etc.; the journals, memoirs, proceedings, transactions, etc., of societies; and numbered monographic series. Newspapers, such as *The Spy and Spirit of the Age, The*

Democratic Sledge Hammer, or the longer-lived *Rolling Stone,* are defined as publications issued on newsprint and containing general news coverage. (*InfoWorld, The Chronicle of Higher Education,* and similar newsprint publications containing special subject matter are not considered newspapers.) Nontextual serials (sound recordings or the new magazines on diskettes, such as *Wheels for the Mind* and *Uptime*) may be cataloged either in the serials format or the format appropriate to the material.

Sound Recordings

The LC-MARC music format is divided into two OCLC-MARC formats, sound recordings and scores, which together represent 4.86% of the records in the database. The sound recordings format (2.84% of the database) encompasses oral-history recordings and interviews, as well as more typical musical recordings. Here, the new technology of compact discs mingles with player-piano and organ rolls. Here, Charlie Parker still jams, opera buffs compare the arias of Jussi Bjoerling with those of Luciano Pavarotti or Placido Domingo, and Prairie Home Companion (like love) never dies.

Bach cantata from a facsimile of the Well-Tempered Clavier, *Book 2, The Ohio State University Libraries. The original is in the Prussian State Library.*

Audiovisual Materials

Records in the audiovisual format (2.38% of the database) include conventional motion pictures, filmstrips, slides, transparencies, and videorecordings. This format also covers three-dimensional materials, such as electronic toys and calculators, models, dioramas, games, and kits or packages of more than one medium designed for use as a unit (unless one medium predominates).

OCLC #3951744 catalogs *Fiddle-de-de,* one of the more unusual forms of this medium, which "presents an experiment in film animation, by painting [directly] on [the] film, in which the violin music of the sound track is interpreted by a flow of colors on the screen."

Music Scores

The music scores format is one of two OCLC-MARC formats representing the LC-MARC music format (sound recordings is the other). This format (2.02% of the records in the database) covers music in print form (including scores and broadsides), manuscripts of music (originals and reproductions or copies), songbooks with words only, books of musical studies and exercises (what struggling pianist can forget Czerny?), score theses, and microform publications of music. Like the sound recordings that carry the music that the scores represent, scores cover the range of form of composition (anthems to waltzes), providing musical notation for everything from the alto saxophone to the zither (a two-volume set of exercises—shades of Czerny). Although music scores are usually in conventional staff notation, the shape-note conventions of the Southern Harmony and similar hymnals can be found, too.

Clip from "Partners of the Tide," produced by Eastern Film Corp. of Providence, c. 1915, based on novel of same name by Joseph C. Lincoln. Film Collection, Rhode Island Historical Society.

Maps

Atlases, which are considered books, are the only type of cartographic material not encompassed by the maps format. Published maps and manuscripts of maps; globes; map theses; microform publications of maps; aeronautical, navigational, and celestial charts; and the LANDSAT images of Earth are all among the 1.19% of the records in the database cataloged in this format.

Maps may be in special formats, such as Braille, blueprints, relief models, or even novelties like playing cards or map puzzles. OCLC #8389657 and #12612431 represent two of the puzzle maps held by the Geography and Map Division of the Library of Congress. A variety of prime meridians (Greenwich, Paris, Philadelphia, and Washington, D.C., among them) may be used, hearkening to ancient times when the frame of reference of any map was whatever was most important to the mapmaker. (All roads *did* sometimes lead to Rome or Athens, or even to New York or Pewaukee—as in the modern-day *New Yorker* magazine cover and one of many paraphrases of it.) Many projection schemes are used to transform some segment(s) of the globe to a flat plane, including the cartographic valentine—the heart-shaped Werner equal-area projection developed by Johann Werner, a contemporary of Columbus.

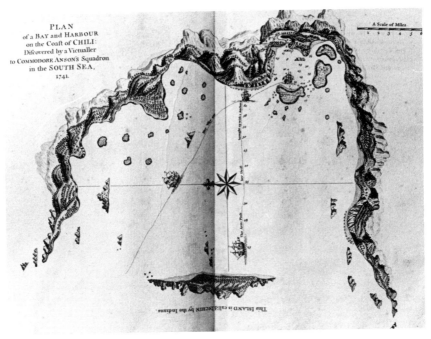

One of the maps of the coast of South America in George Anson's A Voyage Around the World, from the William F. Charters South Seas Collection at Butler, University. Anson traveled to the South Seas and South America in 1740–1744.

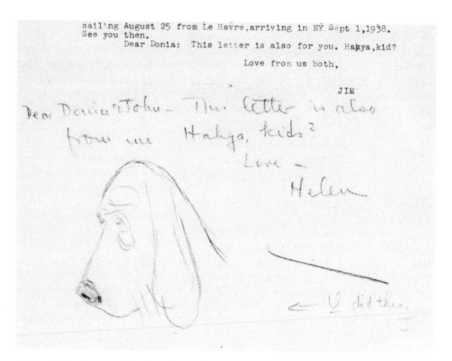

One of the famous Thurber dogs, from a 1938 letter of James and Helen Thurber in the James Thurber Collection, Division of Special Collections, The Ohio State University Libraries.

Archives and Manuscripts

Although probably representing the greatest bulk of material, records in the manuscripts format constitute the smallest percentage of the database (0.40%). For example, OCLC #9635542 catalogs 170 boxes of the personal research collection of Cornelius Ryan. OCLC #6011768 describes 35 cubic feet of correspondence by U.S. Representative Robert Crosser (1874–1957) of Cleveland, Ohio. OCLC #9792474 catalogs 175 cubic feet of material, in 119 boxes, comprising the papers of New Hampshire Governor Charles Tobey from 1933–1953. These three records mention an array of famous correspondents from the New Deal, World War II, and postwar eras.

The format encompasses manuscripts of textual material and reproductions of textual manuscripts—letters, wills, business ledgers, etc. Libraries can enter brief remarks about solicitation (active or not), rules for using their collections, and the last correspondence date, if appropriate.

Machine-readable Data Files

The newest cataloging format, for machine-readable data files (MRDF), comprises 0.10% of the records in the database. MRDF, both the data stored in machine-readable form and the programs used to process that data, accommodates computer programs, including microcomputer and video-game software (OCLC #15213542, *Pac-Man*). The format also covers interactive fiction diskettes (OCLC #15643643, *Trinity*); theses and dissertations in machine-readable form; diskette magazines (OCLC #11215887, *A + Disk Magazine*); and numeric, representational, or text files stored on magnetic tape, punched cards, or disks. A bibliographic record in the MRDF format gives such information as how many programs and diskettes the cataloged item represents; the medium used; what computers can run the program; and the machine language, operating system, and amount of memory needed.

Subsets of the OCLC database—in such subject areas as agriculture, education, science, and technology—are available on compact disc.

William Shakespeare: Growth Industry

William Shakespeare's 36 plays, 2 narrative poems, and 154 sonnets have spawned 16,631 bibliographic records in the OCLC database. Follow the timeline to see the growth of imprints, by year of publication, with Shakespeare as author.

Shakespeare's works have never gone out of print, and OCLC member libraries keep collecting and cataloging them. Since 1984, they have added current and retrospective records for 4,677 imprints to the database.

Shakespeare, of course, is an exception that dramatically illustrates the challenge of dealing with the ever-expanding body of worldwide knowledge and scholarship.

Shakespeare Titles

Number of records entered in the database through 1984

Number of records entered in the database from 1985 to 1988. (During this period, records for Shakespeare titles published between 1965 and 1968 decreased.)

157

107

323

576

1594–1700

1701–1800

Shakespeare and view of the Globe Theatre from The Folger Shakespeare Library. The timeline indicates the number of records for titles by William Shakespeare in the database, categorized by the dates in which the works were originally published.

811 308 678 1,024 952 1,455 1,900 1,484 859 612 598 593 594 714 538 422 1,253 1,427 1,315 1,478 240 1,295 1,290 806 865 855 682 264

1801–1850 1851–1880 1881–1899 1900–1909 1910–1920 1921–1930 1931–1940 1941–1950 1951–1960 1961–1965 1965–1968 1969–1973 1974–1980 1981–1983 1984–1988

The Voyager record in its cover mounted on the spacecraft, courtesy of NASA.

"*[The] Voyager spacecraft has a golden phonograph record in a silver aluminum cover affixed to the outside of its central instrument bay. Instructions for playing the record, written in scientific language, are etched on the cover. A cartridge and stylus, illustrated on the cover, are tucked into the spacecraft nearby. The record is ready to play.*" Carl Sagan, Murmurs of Earth.

The space-age hieroglyphics inscribed on this disk are but one more attempt to convey the experiences of humankind—attempts which, from the Babylonians' impressions in clay to magnetic impressions on tape or disk, are cataloged in the OCLC database and thereby made accessible to libraries and their patrons.

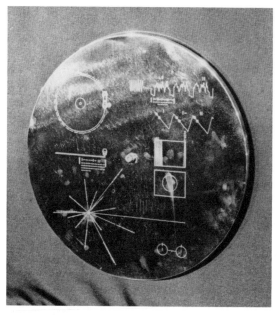

Number of scores by J. S. Bach and sound recordings of those works in the database, categorized by the dates in which the works were originally published or recorded.

Bach Scores and Sound Recordings

Number of records for scores entered in the database through 1984

Number of records for scores entered in the database from 1985 to 1988

Number of records for sound recordings entered in the database through 1984

Number of records for sound recordings entered in the database from 1985 to 1988

314

213

12 98

1

1700–1800

1801–1899

Bach: "Let's Look at the Record."

Johann Sebastian Bach, like Shakespeare, is a case unto himself. Unlike the Bard, whose life's output, though ageless, was not exceptionally prolific, Bach is remarkable for both the quantity and quality of his compositions. The Bach-Werke-Verzeichnis lists 1,080 complete and 189 fragmentary works, in virtually every then-existing medium, which are attributed to this master; the OCLC database records 18,931 separate scores and recordings of those works, plus 91 entries in other media, including one irregular serial.

Some of the increase in the Bach's entries in the 1980s is perhaps attributable to new issues of his works on CD-ROM.

Despite all of the new cataloging work being done, there is one Bach recording that is unlikely ever to be cataloged on the OCLC database. The Voyager spacecraft, launched in 1977, carries a golden disk with recordings of the sights and sounds of humankind in a format especially designed to be interpreted by extraterrestrial life forms—the ultimate gold record! Should Voyager ever find an audience for it, one of the sounds ready to be heard is the Prelude and Fugue in C, No. 1, from Bach's Well Tempered Clavier, Book 2.

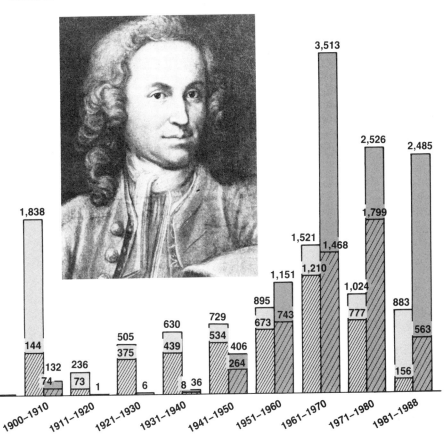

Top 100 Authors in the OCLC Database

Who's the most published author of all time? William Shakespeare, with more than 15,000 titles, tops the list in a computer survey of authors in the OCLC database. Charles Dickens is the number-two author with just under 8,000 titles. Of the two living authors on the list, 1,861 titles are listed for Georges Simenon, and Graham Greene has 1,372.

To make the list, an author had to have at least 1,000 editions of his or her works listed in the OCLC database.

Collectively, the authors' lives encompass time from the 8th century B.C. to the present. They represent a large number of countries, including: America, Belgium, Denmark, England, France, Germany, Greece, India, Ireland, Italy, Norway, Poland, Russia, Samoa, Scotland, and Spain.

Five of the authors (William Faulkner, Anatole France, Rudyard Kipling, George Bernard Shaw, and John Steinbeck) were awarded the Nobel Prize. Faulkner also received the Pulitzer Prize, as did Robert Frost and John Steinbeck.

Only five women are among the top 100: Agatha Christie (no. 33), George Eliot (no. 46), Ellen G. White (no. 74), Jane Austen (no. 76), and George Sand (no. 83).

The top 25 music composers are noted separately. Bach scored the highest, with approximately 17,640 database records to his credit. Mozart occupied second chair with 17,150. Beethoven was an heroic third with 13,622. A distant fourth was Brahms, with 8,133. Sorry, no rock composers even came close.

Top 100 Authors

1 William Shakespeare	22 Dante Alighieri
2 Charles Dickens	23 Jakob Grimm
3 Sir Walter Scott	24 Plato
4 Johann Goethe	25 Edgar Allan Poe
5 Aristotle	26 Burt Standish
6 Alexandre Dumas	27 William Thackeray
7 Robert Louis Stevenson	28 Nathaniel Hawthorne
8 Mark Twain	29 John Milton
9 Marcus Cicero	30 John Ruskin
10 Honore de Balzac	31 Leo Tolstoy
11 Rudyard Kipling	32 Virgil
12 Victor Hugo	33 Agatha Christie
13 Washington Irving	34 Joseph Conrad
14 James Fenimore Cooper	35 Henry Wadsworth Longfellow
15 Daniel Defoe	36 Friedrich von Schiller
16 Martin Luther	37 Jules Verne
17 Miguel de Cervantes Saavedra	38 Sir Arthur Conan Doyle
18 Erle Stanley Gardner	39 Horace
19 Homer	40 Henry James
20 Voltaire	41 Edward Bulwer Lytton
21 Hans Christian Andersen	42 Moliere

43 Lewis Carroll
44 Oliver Goldsmith
45 George Bernard Shaw
46 George Eliot
47 Oscar Wilde
48 Thomas Carlyle
49 Ralph Waldo Emerson
50 Thomas Hardy
51 Samuel Johnson
52 Karl Marx
53 Georges Simenon
54 John Dryden
55 Wilhelm Grimm
56 Ovid
57 Alfred Lord Tennyson
58 H. G. Wells
59 Feodor Dostoyevsky
60 Euripides
61 Jack London
62 Guy de Maupassant
63 Johathan Swift
64 Emile Zola
65 Jean Jacques Rousseau
66 Robert Browning
67 John Bunyan
68 Lord Byron
69 Geoffrey Chaucer
70 William Faulkner
71 Andrew Lang
72 Vladimir Lenin
73 Alexander Pope
74 Ellen G. White
75 Isaac Asimov
76 Jane Austen
77 Robert Burns
78 Friedrich Engels
79 Anatole France
80 Benjamin Franklin
81 Charles Lamb
82 D. H. Lawrence
83 George Sand
84 Sophocles
85 Anthony Trollope
86 John Wesley
87 John Steinbeck

88 Pedro Calderon de la Barca
89 Robert Frost
90 Graham Greene
91 Hippocrates
92 Oliver Wendell Holmes
93 Henrik Ibsen
94 Thomas Mann
95 Lope de Vega
96 Jacob Abbott
97 Aeschylus
98 Aesop
99 Nick Carter
100 C. K. Chesterton

Top 25 Composers

1 Johann Sebastian Bach
2 Wolfgang Amadeus Mozart
3 Ludwig van Beethoven
4 Johannes Brahms
5 Joseph Haydn
6 Franz Schubert
7 George Handel
8 Peter Tchaikovsky
9 Robert Schumann
10 Richard Wagner
11 Guiseppe Verdi
12 Frederic Chopin
13 Franz Liszt
14 Felix Mendelssohn
15 Claude Debussy
16 Antonio Vivaldi
17 Antonin Dvorak
18 Sergei Prokofiev
19 Richard Strauss
20 Maurice Ravel
21 Igor Stravinsky
22 Bela Bartok
23 Gioacchino Rossini
24 Giacomo Puccini
25 Sergei Rachmaninoff

About the Special Collections

Through the ages, libraries have been collectors of books, but even within this tradition there are exceptions—the special collections. The American Library Association defines a special collection as:

> ". . . material of a certain form, on a certain subject, of a certain period, or gathered together for some particular reason, in a library. . . ."

Like all collectors, libraries tend to specialize in certain types of items or in materials with a theme but, instead of quilts or "anything with frogs," the specialities are more likely to be Orientalia or works of fiction written by doctors. And, like most collectors, libraries are always interested in expanding these collections, in part by letting others know what they have and are interested in.

Unlike a good many collectors, libraries keep very careful records describing these acquisitions—their local catalogs. In addition, many such collections are cataloged among the millions of items which make up the OCLC database—the catalog of catalogs.

These special collections are as diverse as the libraries holding them. OCLC members include academic, public, corporate, research, and government libraries, with particular interests in medicine and the health sciences, law, English and American drama of the 19th century, music, and Eastern European publications, to cite but a few areas of emphasis. The information in this publication, like that in the database, was contributed by the libraries themselves, with the intention of making these special collections ever more widely known.

This guide will be revised periodically. If you would like to share information about your library's special collections with the library community, please send the appropriate description for inclusion in the next edition and, if possible, illustrations or photographs of special items to:

OCLC
Special Collections Guide, MC 123
6565 Frantz Road
Dublin, Ohio 43017–0702

The Special Collections

This popularized guide to the special collections cataloged in the OCLC database is arranged alphabetically by state. Within each state, entries are arranged alphabetically by institution (disregarding the phrase *University of*) and include each institution's OCLC symbol. A subject index is in the back of the guide. OCLC member libraries supplied the information about their special collections.

Birmingham Southern College (ABB)
Birmingham, AL

H. Halsey Townes Collection of Alabama History & Alabama Authors. Consists of 1,206 titles in 1,412 volumes. Books may only be used within the library.

Arkansas State University (ASU)
State University, AR

Cass S. Hough Aeronautical Collection. Described as "the single most important and valuable collection of aviation materials in private hands." The Hough Collection consists of approximately 7,000 collector's items and some 3,000 monograph and serial titles. A complete collection of *Der Flieger,* a training camp newspaper published for the German air force in World War I, is included. The collection is basically a 20th century one, but pre-20th century books on the topics of balloons and rockets were also acquired.

Azusa Pacific University (CAP)
Azusa, CA

Special Collections Library. A research collection of 15,000 books, periodicals, manuscripts, photographs, and audiotapes relating to the history and culture of California and the American West. Special emphases include the Gold Rush, the Church in the Far West, General George A. Custer, and the history of the Los Angeles basin. In addition, there are collections of literary first editions, materials on Presidents Adams and Lincoln, and numerous examples of fine, that is, high quality, noncommercial printing.

California State University, Fullerton (CFI)
Fullerton, CA

History of Cartography. Includes rare and antiquarian, manuscript and printed, geographical maps, from the earliest times through the 19th century, as well as reference and scholarly works in book, pamphlet, and journal form. The collection consists of more than 1,470 rare maps and approximately 4,300 volumes representing about 1,600 titles. The Western Association of Map Libraries cites this collection as being ". . . recognized by curators for its care, preservation, and organization and serves as one of the world's superior models for collections of rare maps."

The James S. Copley Library (JSC)
La Jolla, CA

The library contains approximately 2,400 autograph letters and documents, the vast majority of which pertain to the American Revolutionary War period, but correspondence of Mark Twain, John Charles Fremont, Jessie Benton Fremont, and Benito Juarez is included. The library also contains 10,000 volumes pertaining to these same subjects as well as covering various aspects in the settlement of California and the West.

Beethoven's Pastorale, *from the Ira Brilliant Center for Beethoven Studies, San Jose State University.*

Golden West College (CGW)
Huntington Beach, CA

Golden West College TeleMedia Productions Collection. Contains 23 titles and 23 volumes of campus-produced videotaped instructional programs dealing with a variety of topics including how to use a reference collection, how to operate a light microscope, and how to prepare for a successful job interview.

Institute of Transportation Studies (CBT)
Berkeley, CA

This intermodal, interdisciplinary collection contains 102,000 books, reports, pamphlets, and bound serials and an additional 22,000 reports in microfiche. Since 1974, almost all federally sponsored reports on transportation have been acquired as part of the library's role as a U.S. Dept. of Transportation depository.

Loma Linda University (LLU)
Loma Linda, CA

Adventist Heritage Collection. Although this collection of approximately 12,000 monographs relates to various Adventist denominations, special emphasis is on the Seventh-day Adventist Church. The collection includes extensive Advent Christian and Millerite Adventist works as well as holdings of smaller Adventist bodies. Also collected are materials pertaining to 19th century water cure, phrenology, and duplicates of many volumes originally found in the personal library of Ellen G. White, cofounder of the Seventh-day Adventist Church. Audiovisual materials and unpublished manuscripts also comprise a portion of the collection.

San Jose State University (CSJ)
San Jose, CA

Ira F. Brilliant Center for Beethoven Studies Collection. Officially open for only a year, the Center owns more than 350 first, later 19th-century, and modern editions of Beethoven's scores and over 700 books about Beethoven and related subjects. For those interested in Beethoven's published scores, the Center can provide at least one, and often multiple editions of nearly every opus, most of which were published in the first half of the 19th century. First editions, supplemented by 30 or so photocopies from the Library of Congress and other collections, currently number more than 100. The scores may be studied and compared at the Center or photocopies can be ordered at 15¢ per page. On open shelves are the new critical edition being published by Henle for the Beethoven-archiv in Bonn, as well as the "complete" 19th century edition of Breitkopf and Hartel and the supplement to that Gesamtausgabe edited by Willy Hess. The Center's collection of biographical writings covers more than 150 years and is a nearly complete compilation of Beethoven biographies published as monographs. A donation from the *San Jose Mercury News* enables patrons to enjoy a growing collection of recordings on the Center's stereo system, including the piano sonatas (many on the fortepiano) and string quartets, as well as the Beethoven Bicentennial Collection issued by Deutsche Grammaphone. Excluding items too worn or rare to travel, all books are available on interlibrary loan once they have been cataloged on OCLC.

University of California, Berkeley (CUY)
Berkeley, CA

Government Documents. Over 17,000 monographic titles, including many unique records for California legislative hearings. The documents collection is one of the few in the nation which has received full cataloging since its inception.

Latin American studies, North American exploration, and works by and about Hermann Hesse are also areas of strength.

University of California, Davis (CUX)
Davis, CA

Loren D. Carlson Health Sciences Library Special Collection. Includes works of interest in the history of veterinary medicine. Among the collection are a 1618 edition of the first work of veterinary anatomy based on Vesalian principles, the Carlo Ruini *Anatomia del cavallo, infermita, et svoi rimedii,* and two copies of Philippe LaFosse *Cours d'hippiatrique, ou, Traite complet de medicine des chevaux* (1772), one of which has hand-tinted plates. Except for a few serials, the entire collection is represented in the OCLC database.

University of California, Irvine (CUI)
Irvine, CA

The Emma D. Menninger Collection. Over 2,000 books, pamphlets, and serial volumes in horticulture, with an intensive focus on orchid literature of the 19th and 20th centuries.

The Rene Wellek Collection of the History of Criticism. Works selected by Professor Wellek (author of *A History of Modern Criticism*) from his personal library, which he considers essential for the study of the history of criticism and literary theory, with greatest emphasis on the period from the 18th century to the present. Over 3,150 volumes cataloged.

University of California, San Diego (CUS)
La Jolla, CA

Herbert R. Southworth Spanish Civil War Collection. This collection constitutes the largest single body of Spanish Civil War materials known to scholars, with a high percentage of rare and unique items not represented in any other American or European library. The collection brings together a wide variety of publications produced by the major factions contending for power in Spain before and during the Civil War and is also strong in publications covering the period of ostracism of the monarchy following the War. The collection consists of over 10,000 monographs and pamphlets and 600 serial titles. By the end of 1983, approximately one-third of the collection had been entered into the OCLC database.

The Colorado College (COC)
Colorado Springs, CO

The John A. Carruthers Collection. Includes more than 70 volumes by Charles Dickens, including many first editions in the original parts. The oldest book in the 200-volume collection is a 1491 edition of Dante's *La Divina Commedia.* Also included is the first complete translation of Boccaccio's *Decameron,* a first edition of Milton's *Paradise Regain'd* (1671), an early edition (1699) of *Paradise Lost,* and numerous 17th century editions of Latin classics.

Justice Chess Collection. A 300-volume collection of rare books on the game of chess given to Colorado College Library in 1957 was cataloged for the first time during 1982. The collection, given to the library by Philip S. Justice of Denver, includes 162 titles, several rare 16th and 17th century items, and numerous periodicals. The collection represents a wide range of historical bindings and a number of examples of fine printing from various countries.

Denver Conservative Baptist Seminary (CBS)
Denver, CO

The Library of Ancient Middle Eastern History. Given to the seminary by Ronald Sammons, this collection contains scholarly works in the area of Middle East archeology and history, many of which are rare and out of print. There are approximately 4,000 titles, plus many back runs of journals. Wide interest in this collection is evidenced by the number of interlibrary loan requests received for these books.

Denver Public Library (DPL)
Denver, CO

Approximately 4,000 titles dealing with American Indians and Colorado have been cataloged online, with an estimated 1,900 additional titles in progress.

Loretto Heights College (COL)
Denver, CO

Research Center on Women. The center is one of the oldest of its kind in the U.S. and has materials from the 1700s to the present.

University of Colorado at Boulder (COD)
Boulder, CO

The Kelmscott Press Collection. Another collection acquired from Samuel Goldman, consisting of almost every work printed at the famous English press in the 1980s.

The Limited Edition Club Collection. This collection was obtained from Samuel Goldman, a local collector, and contains virtually all of the works of the Limited Edition Club from its inception to the mid-1970s.

The John Masefield Collection. This collection of approximately 100 works contains many of the major and minor works of John Masefield, the English poet, in whatever edition printed.

The Mountaineering Collection. The core of this collection, which is partially cataloged on OCLC, was formed by two Denver men, John Jerome Hart and Frank Campbell. In addition, the collection has become a depository for the American Alpine Club's duplicates. The collection consists of books, manuscripts, photographs, maps, etc. Anything related to mountaineering, no matter where in the world, is accepted into the collection.

University of Denver (DVP)
Denver, CO

Margaret Husted Culinary Collection. Consists of 7,385 bound volumes, plus periodicals, pamphlets, advertising booklets featuring recipes and food information, a collection of almanacs, and other printed ephemera. While emphasizing American regional cooking, there are many books devoted to cooking and food throughout the world. There are works on all specialties of cooking, a useful reference library, and 20 manuscripts, English and American, ranging from 1695 through the early 20th century. In addition to standard American texts on gastronomy, there are many curiosities of pre-1860 English and American cookbooks. Subject headings in the collection run from artichokes to yogurt.

University of Southern Colorado (COS)
Pueblo, CO

American Musical Heritage Collection. Over 6,000 phonodiscs, ranging from Patti and Caruso to the Beatles, purchased from the estate of a local collector whose activities and catholic tastes spanned 50 years of recordings. Included in the collection are many 78s, both 10- and 12-inch, with a heavy concentration in the 1940s.

Central Connecticut State University (CTB)
New Britain, CT

Walter Hart Blumenthal Collection. This collection consists of books, articles, and unpublished manuscripts spanning 40 years.

Elihu Burritt Collection. Books by and about the "learned blacksmith and advocate of peace." In addition, there is one foot of Burritt's correspondence.

Frederic Goudy Collection. Approximately 215 books, pamphlets, and broadsides printed at the Village Press. Partially entered onto OCLC.

Polish Heritage Collection. Over 3,800 titles on Poland in English and Polish; 2,500 titles have been entered on OCLC.

Bruce Rogers Collection. 255 books and pamphlets designed or printed by Mr. Rogers between 1895–1956.

Mark Twain Collection. 300 volumes by or about Mark Twain. Many first editions of his writings, including several books from his library.

Daniel Webster Collection. Over 100 volumes of Webster's writings and speeches.

Connecticut College (CTL)
New London, CT

The Downs Angling Collection. Approximately 1,500 nineteenth and twentieth century titles on fish and angling, including many rarities.

The Gildersleeve Collection of 19th and Early 20th Century Children's Literature. Cataloging is still in process and will cover approximately 2,000 titles when completed.

The Rockville Public Library (RLP)
Vernon, CT

Rockville/Vernon Local History Collection. 111 titles comprised of newspaper clippings, eyewitness accounts of local events, town ordinances, reports, and photo records of the area dating back to the 1800s.

The University of Connecticut (UCW)
Storrs, CT

Alternative Press Collection. An active collection of books, pamphlets, and journals of an alternative nature, being cataloged on a continuing basis and now into the thousands of items. The original collection related to the student movements of the 1960s, subsequent additions have changed the focus to current political and social problems. Also included are American socialist and communist pamphlets of 1920–1950.

Arjona Collection. 291 volumes from the library of Jaime H. Arjona, internationally known expert on Lope de Vega, consist chiefly of Lope de Vega's works in various editions, including microfilm copies of a number of Lope's holograph plays.

Belgian Revolution Collection. 1,087 books and pamphlets relating to the establishment of the modern state of Belgium, 1830–1839; Belgian and Dutch imprints.

Camoes Collection. Primary and secondary material about Luis de Camoes (1524?–1580). Chiefly in Portuguese. Most of the 350 titles have been cataloged on OCLC.

Children's Literature Collection. A small research collection of about 1,000 titles of the period 1840–1920, with emphasis on 1860–1900 (the period often ignored

Pen-and-ink bookplate art for Rudolph Valentino by William Cameron Menzies, from the Exlibris Collection, University of Connecticut.

by other collectors). Illustrated material is emphasized. A collection is currently being built of contemporary children's illustrated books, with an emphasis on Connecticut authors and illustrators and nearly all are being cataloged on OCLC.

Chile Collection. A growing collection covering the history and politics of Chile from the 16th century to the present; the bulk of the collection covers 1810–1940. More than 2,500 titles have been cataloged on OCLC.

Columbia University Contributions to Education Collection. Most of the books included in this microfiche set were originally theses presented to Columbia University between 1905–1951.

Connecticut Historic Preservation Collection. Includes archeological and historical register information; 300 archeological survey reports will be input on OCLC.

Exlibris Collection. The collection contains 250 library reference books, some periodicals, and several thousand examples of bookplates. The reference books are being cataloged on OCLC.

French Political Pamphlets. 913 pamphlets concerned with the historical and political events of the Bourbon Restoration, 1815–1835, plus some works dealing with the Revolutionary and Napoleonic periods. Titles cataloged to date are virtually all original input.

Pierce Welsh Gaines Collection of Americana. The collection, chiefly devoted to the Federalist period of U.S. history, 1789–1809, contains about 4,500 items of primary and secondary sources. The collection also concentrates on the emergence of the two-party political system in America.

Italian Risorgimento Collection. Primary and secondary source materials in book, pamphlets, periodicals, and some 6,000 broadsides, covering the period of the unification of Italy, 1789–1870.

Kays Collection. 252 books and 2,612 periodical issues on the breeding and care of horses, horseback riding, and horse racing. There are popular, scholarly, and scientific works and some juvenile works, covering all aspects of the horse. The collection is being cataloged on OCLC.

Paul Laumonier Collection of French Renaissance Literature. Numerous rare books of the 16th and 17th centuries, with emphasis on Pierre Ronsard and the Pleiade. The notes of Paul Laumonier (1867–1949), an internationally known Ronsard scholar and editor, are found throughout his books. Also includes some of Laumonier's manuscripts and note materials. The collection is partially cataloged on OCLC.

Literary Manuscripts and Archives. A collection on manuscripts of post-modern writers, principally the poet Charles Olson and his associates. Some of the smaller manuscript collections have been cataloged on OCLC, including the Catherine Seelye-Olson/Pound papers, William K. Costley papers, and the Warren-Debs-Sinclair papers.

Madrid Collection. Over 2,000 books, pamphlets, and broadsides relating to the history of Madrid. The collection was formed by Jose Luis Oliva Escribano of Madrid as the basis for his extensive bibliography, *Bibliografia de Madrid y su Provincia* (OCLC #344139). The collection is being cataloged on OCLC.

Medina Collection. 307 volumes of the bibliographical and historical works of Chilean scholar and bibliographer Jose Toribio Medina (1852–1930), as well as secondary works about him. Virtually all of his works are first editions, a number of them quite rare. The collection is partially cataloged on OCLC.

Natural History Collection. The collection consists of rare and valuable books about birds, flowers, and butterflies and contains beautiful colorplate illustrations. The floral material is particularly strong in herbals. Some of the collection is cataloged on OCLC.

Puerto Rican Collection. More than 2,000 volumes of source materials (books, pamphlets, government documents, and some periodicals) on the social, economic, political, and literary history of Puerto Rico during the late 19th and early 20th centuries. The earlier materials deal more with the socio-historical evolution of Puerto Rico; later items focus on the island's social and economic conditions. The collection was assembled by four generations of the Geigel family of Puerto Rico. All of the collection (excluding the government documents and periodicals) is cataloged on OCLC.

Edwin Way Teale Collection. The diaries, journals, and correspondence of the late Pulitzer prize-winning naturalist, all the manuscripts for his extensive writings, and thousands of photographs. Also 150 published monographs, including all his published writings and a number of books presented to him by noted authors.

Henry Francis du Pont Winterthur Museum Library (DLH)
Winterthur, DE

Printed Book and Periodical Collection. This collection has been developed for research in the history of American art and material culture to 1914 and its British and Continental background. There are over 70,000 bound volumes in the collection; 300 periodical subscriptions are maintained. Since 1980, 12,500 titles, representing new acquisitions chiefly, have been cataloged on the OCLC system. Approximately 2,000 titles will be added to the collection each year. Smaller collections within this larger one are the Edward Deming Andrews Memorial Shaker Collection, the Waldron Phoenix Belknap, Jr. Research Library of American Painting, and the Trade Catalogue Collection.

American Association of Retired Persons (NGR)
Washington, DC

The National Gerontology Resource Center contains approximately 10,000 titles on middle age and aging, with emphasis on retirement planning, public policy, health care services, and social security. About 1,000 aging-related titles are added each year.

The George Washington University (DGW)
Washington, DC

Carnegie Collection. In 1950, this collection of 70,000 books, pamphlets, and documents belonging to the Library of the Carnegie Endowment for International Peace was sold to George Washington University. At that time, an evaluation officer from the Library of Congress described the collection as being ''so carefully and consistently assembled that it has come to be considered one of the most authoritative sources for the study of international questions.'' Founded in 1910 by Andrew Carnegie, the Endowment was charged by its creator with ''hastening the abolition of international war, the foulest blot upon our civilization.'' Toward that goal, the Library comprehensively collected titles from many nations and in many languages, including documents of foreign governments, texts about the events and individuals that were to determine national futures, and pamphlets varying in subject matter from predictable political and social propaganda literature to such still timely issues as women's rights, disarmament, and economic theory.

Georgetown University (DGU)
Washington, DC

American Catholic Sermon Collection. Some 451 manuscript sermons and fragments by 43 preachers, including 55 by Archbishop John Carroll, date from before 1723 to 1800. Since only a handful of American Catholic sermons were published during the 18th century and none before 1786, these manuscripts allow significant research in the fields of literary, historical, and theological interest.

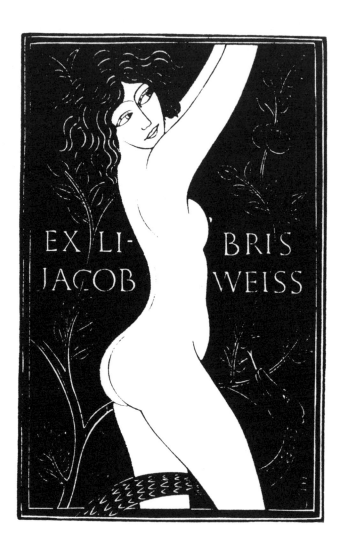

Wood engraving bookplate art by Eric Gill, from the Exlibris Collection, University of Connecticut.

American Heritage School Dictionary Corpus. The 351 linear feet of materials in this collection record the development of this first dictionary to utilize computer technology. Included are the file of books used to locate citations, punch cards and printed citations, and various magnetic tape files (including the "word frequency" listings that were the basis for the *American Heritage Word Frequency Book.*

David Rankin Barbee Papers. The papers include files compiled during the early 1900s by historian and journalist Barbee focusing on Lincoln and the Civil War, particularly events leading to Lincoln's assassination. Barbee tracked down people who were near the events in question, making the files valuable to students of the assassination. Material on Confederate spy Rose O'Neil Greenhow is also included.

Russell J. Bowen Collection. This growing collection numbers over 6,600 titles on intelligence, spying, covert activities, and related phenomena assembled by Col. Bowen. Access to the first 5,300 titles is facilitated by the published bibliography of the collection, *Scholar's Guide to Intelligence Literature.* OCLC #9595527.

Flaccus-Masters Archive. Correspondence and research files developed by poet Kimball Flaccus in process of writing a biography of Edgar Lee Masters. Besides letters from Masters and virtually all of his acquaintances, the collection includes correspondence of Upton Sinclair, Conrad Aiken, John Dos Passos, and the widows of Vachel Lindsay and Sherwood Anderson. The collection is complemented by books by and about Masters and a number of his letters in other collections (for example, correspondence with Milton Cushing).

Haggerty Collection. Some 2,000 World War I British regimental unit histories and personal narratives assembled by Louis C. Haggerty correspond to a similar collection of American unit histories Haggerty donated to Princeton University.

Harry L. Hopkins Papers. The Hopkins papers consist of 26 linear feet of the personal archives of Franklin Roosevelt's most trusted advisor. They include appointment books, diaries, drafts of Hopkins' speeches and memoranda, and extensive correspondence with family and friends, including President and Mrs. Roosevelt, Averell Harriman, George C. Marshall, Carl Sandburg, Felix Frankfurter, Dwight Eisenhower, Harold Ickes, and Rexford Tugwell. The papers help document virtually all facets of Hopkins' career, both as chief architect of the New Deal and head of the Lend-Lease program and as a major policy maker in the matter of Roosevelt's negotiations with Stalin and Churchill.

Ernest Larue Jones Collection. Some 1,500 photographs mounted in seven volumes relate the early history of American aviation. The photos were taken or collected by Jones primarily between 1907–1915 when he was editor of the pioneer technical journal *Aeronautics.*

McCarthy Historical Project Archive. Records of Eugene McCarthy's national campaign office, supplemented by selected records of state offices, paid television and radio ads, speech and release files, and written and oral history narratives by many of the most active participants in the campaign comprise this archive, which is among the largest collections of records of any American political primary campaign. The archive is supplemented by numerous collections bearing on the 1968 campaign, including the records of the Women for McCarthy group, papers of journalist William Stout and historian J. Herman Schauinger, and papers of Senator McCarthy's further attempts at the Presidency in 1972 and 1976. The McCarthy collections total nearly 545 linear feet.

Modern Fine Printing. Nearly 1,000 modern "press books," principally American, include works from virtually all the major American private presses (Elston, Cranbrook, Village, Cummington, the Grabhorns, Pennyroyal). Over 200 examples of Peter Beilenson's works (Peter Pauper Press, Walpole Printing Office, Press of the Blue-behinded Ape) are held. The output of Stephen Hurlbut's St. Alban's Press is held almost completely. There are also examples from the great English presses. **The Riedel Collec-**

tion subset includes the bulk of Eric Gill's private press books and a long run of publications by H.D.C. Pepler's St. Dominic's Press.

Panama and the Canal. Papers of Tomas Herran; Earl Harding; the Panama Canal Subcommittee on Merchant Marine and Fisheries, U.S. House of Representatives and Rep. Leonor K. Sullivan, chairwoman of the committee 1955-1971; and Capt. Miles P. DuVal, Jr., author of *Cadiz to Cathay* (1940), comprise the bulk of a number of collections relating to the history of the Canal. The collections date from the abortive Hay-Herran Treaty of 1903, which would have provided for American construction of the Canal through what was then part of Colombia and cover the 1903 revolution in Panama, Theodore Roosevelt's libel suit against Joseph Pulitzer and *The* [N.Y.] *World,* the Panama Canal Treaty that transferred authority over the Canal to Panama, and Panamanian affairs, Canal policy, and tolls circa 1947–1960.

Parsons Collection. Nearly 500 works by Catholic authors printed in the U.S. between 1720 and 1830. Includes the only known copy of the first American Catholic directory (1817). The collection is supplemented by works in the Woodstock Theological Library, including the first edition of *The Book of Mormon* (1830) and the only known copy of the 1825 Bardstown *Catechism.*

Quigley Photographic Archive and Deposit Collections. These two collections comprise the photo "morgue" of Quigley Publications, active under various titles since 1915 in motion picture industry trade publishing, plus the most complete runs extant of these titles: *Motion Picture Herald* and its antecedents, 1915–1972; *Motion Picture Daily,* 1930–1972; *International Motion Picture (Television) Almanac,* 1930 to date; and *Fame,* 1937–1970. The morgue is an assemblage of publicity photos that includes producers, directors, animators, and other industry notables as well as actors and actresses. The approximately 55,000 black-and-white photos and 3,500 negatives date from about 1906 to 1972. Smaller files of photos are devoted to motion picture studios, theaters, and equipment. The publications collection includes a partial rough subject index to *Motion Picture Herald* and a complete card file index to film reviews published in *Motion Picture Daily.*

Shea Collection. Nearly 10,000 books, journals, newspapers, and pamphlets make up the library of American Catholic historian John Gilmary Shea. The collection is strong in 16th–18th century works relating to the exploration of Canada and the Spanish Southwest, including one of two known copies of Juan de Montoya's *Relacion* (1602). Part of the collection, but uncataloged, is a comprehensive collection of American Catholic 19th century pamphlets, including virtually complete sets of records of diocesan synods and pastoral letters.

Zalles Celtic Collection. The main thrust of this collection of over 1,000 books and journals is Irish language, history, and culture, but important subsets of the collection relate to Breton, Cornish, Scots Gaelic, and Welsh. Special strengths include publications of a number of the learned societies that have specialized in Celtic culture and linguistics.

Smithsonian Institution (SMI)
Washington, DC

The Dibner Collection. This collection consists of over 1,600 scientific manuscripts extending from the 13th to the 20th century and includes letters and texts by Galileo, Darwin, Newton, Einstein, and other major figures in the history of western thought.

National Museum of Design. The Branch Library for the Cooper-Hewitt Museum was founded in 1897 as part of the Cooper Union Museum for the Arts of Decoration, a teaching collection for design students enrolled at the Cooper Union for the Advancement of Science and Art. The present library contains 35,000 books, periodicals, and exhibition and collection catalogs relating to the history of design, the decorative arts, ornamentation, and textiles. Other subject areas include architecture and interior design, gardening and landscape architecture, theatre and costume design, world's fairs, travel, royal celebrations, graphic arts, and the art of the book. The rare book collection contains approximately 3,000 volumes. Most are notable for their illustrations, and many were used as pattern books for designers and craftsmen in the decorative arts.

U.S. Department of Commerce Bureau of the Census (CBU)
Washington, DC

The Census Collection. U.S. census reports dated back to 1790. U.S. census reports of population, housing, construction, governments, manufacturers, transportation, and business are cataloged. More than 1,000 U.S. census titles and about 1,200 foreign census titles have been added, and the Bureau of the Census is continually adding both current and retrospective titles.

Embry-Riddle Aeronautical University (FER)
Daytona Beach, FL

Special Collection. An assemblage of unique materials specific to the development of the aviation industry, consisting of 2,200 volumes representing 2,000 titles.

The Florida State University (FDA)
Tallahassee, FL

The French Revolution and Napoleon Collection. Consists of approximately 13,000 volumes, with an estimated 6,000 titles cataloged on OCLC. Included are materials from the British, French, Spanish, and German viewpoints in a variety of formats, including documents, laws, military histories, individual battle accounts, memoirs, maps, manuscripts, books on clothing and uniforms, etc.

University of South Florida (FHM)
Tampa, FL

19th Century American Literature. Approximately 6,300 volumes have been cataloged on OCLC; approximately 1,200 are awaiting cataloging. Among the authors represented in this special collection whose works have been cataloged are: Timothy Shay Arthur, approximately 200 volumes; Horatio Alger, approximately 400 volumes; Oliver Optic (William T. Adams), approximately 100 volumes; and Edward Sylvester Ellis, 200 volumes.

The Henty Collection. An extensive collection of the works of George Alfred Henty, a popular English author of adventure stories for boys, and Hentyana formed mainly from the merger of those items collected by William B. Poage and James Baird Herndon. Approximately 200 titles have been cataloged and about as many volumes remain to be cataloged.

University of Tampa (FUT)
Tampa, FL

The Florida Military Collection. The collection comprises one of the largest private libraries of books and documents on military subjects in the southeastern U.S. It contains approximately 11,000 books, plus many newspapers, magazines, maps, pamphlets, records, and correspondence (military memorabilia), realia (artifacts such as medals, inert bombs, photographs, bronze grave markers, boots, swords, sabres, rifles, flags, and uniforms of various services, etc.) Also included are autographed copies of books and letters from historical figures, military, political, and literary. The project is a joint effort of the university and the Association of the U.S. Army.

Abraham Baldwin Agricultural College (GTM)
Tifton, GA

Georgiana Collection. Consists of books about Georgia and/or Georgians or books written by Georgians.

Armstrong State College (GAC)
Savannah, GA

The Minis Collection. Approximately 900 titles, concentrating on the works of Georgia, and more specifically, Savannah authors. Almost every one of Conrad Aiken's works are included in the collection. Most of Mr. Aiken's books are either first editions or autographed copies. The Minis Room also contains a limited number of books dealing with Savannah history and geography.

Emory University (EMT)
Atlanta, GA

African Christian Periodicals. Consists of more than 200 current and 150 noncurrent serials published by Christian churches and institutions throughout Africa, with special attention to the sub-Saharan countries. Approximately 150 of the current titles have been entered in the OCLC database.

Manning Collection. Includes 3,639 volumes representing 2,718 titles primarily from the personal library of Henry Edward Manning, Cardinal Archbishop of Westminster, whose contributions to education and social work in Great Britain are highly regarded.

Pitts Theology Library is entering into the online catalog a collection of religious theses from Western Europe (chiefly Germany and Scandinavia) printed from about 1600–1800. Ultimate objective is the publication of a bibliography of these Latin materials as an aid to students and scholars in the fields of religion, theology, philosophy, and history. Approximately 450 entries out of a total of 5,500 dissertations have been added to the OCLC database.

Mercer University (MWU)
Macon, GA

Georgia Baptist Historical Collection. Approximately 700 titles, 1,300 volumes. Books, periodicals, and manuscripts on Baptist history, especially in Georgia; includes histories of particular churches and associations, sermons, memoirs, etc. Also included are materials on Mercer University history and Georgia county histories.

National Archives and Records Service (NAR)
Atlanta, GA

Security Collection (JECC). This collection contains President Carter's personal library (i.e., books read and annotated by Jimmy Carter), presentation copies of books by famous authors, and "treasure" books given to Mr. Carter by foreign government and private citizens (e.g., the Louvain Bible, 1553, given to the Carters by King Baudouin I on the occasion of their trip to Belgium).

University of Hawaii at Manoa (HUH)
Honolulu, HI

Hawaiian Collection. Hawaiiana dating back to 1927. Special features include University of Hawaii dissertations and theses and Hawaii state documents. The collection had 35,594 titles in 75,385 volumes as of September 30, 1983.

Pacific Collection. An outstanding collection of Pacifica ranked among the top three in the world. The collection provides research materials for students and faculty in academic programs at the university which focus on the Pacific, as well as for researchers in many disciplines. Included in this collection are materials on Polynesia (excluding Hawaii), Micronesia, and Melanesia. From October 1, 1981 to December 31, 1982, manual cataloging records in the collection were converted into machine-readable form with a grant from the U.S. Department of Education; 14,988 titles were converted on OCLC, of which 8,739 titles (58%) were input into the OCLC database as new records. In addition, 4,280 titles were cataloged since the library joined OCLC in May 1979. At the end of September 1983, this unique collection had 30,945 titles in 46,356 volumes, of which 19,268 titles (62%) were in the OCLC database.

South/Southeast Asia Collection. Thai material in the South/Southeast Asia Collection has been cataloged on OCLC since February 1982. With a federal grant through the National Resource Center for Southeast Asia at the University of Hawaii at Manoa, 1,196 titles were cataloged, of which 924 titles were added to the OCLC database as new records.

American Hospital Association (IHD)
Chicago, IL

Hospital and Health Service Administration Collection. The nation's foremost collection of informational resources on hospital and health services administration consists of more than 40,000 volumes, including works of the Association and its affiliates and subsidiaries. A subset of the general collection is the Ray E. Brown Management Collection, which consists of classic books in the field of management. This joint collection of the American Hospital Association and the American College of Healthcare Executives (AHA/ACHE) consists of 650 volumes. Another subset, the AHA/ACHE Historical Collection, consists of 850 volumes of hospital histories from the 17th–19th centuries and hospital administration texts from the early 20th century.

Aurora University (ICA)
Aurora, IL

Jenks Memorial Collection of Adventual Materials. Materials relating to William Miller and the Millerite Movement of the first half of the 19th century in America, historical materials relating to the Advent Christian Church, and materials of the other Adventist groups which developed from the movement. In addition to general works in Church histories, the collection contains works in Christian theology and ethics, journals and periodicals, books, photographs, charts, homiletical materials, slides, and tapes. The collection contains 1,100 pamphlets.

Bank Marketing Association (IDZ)
Chicago, IL

Golden Coins. Contains 1,329 bank marketing and community affairs case studies submitted by bankers throughout the country for BMA's annual Golden Coin Competition.

Marketing Plans. These 38 student papers from the School of Bank Marketing are proposed plans for marketing projects. The format includes a situation analysis, objectives, and strategies.

Project Reports. Contains 1,115 student papers from the School of Bank Marketing, sponsored by Bank Marketing Association. Project reports may be in two formats: original activities reports which are marketing projects carried out by the students in their own institutions, and research reports which are investigations of some area of bank marketing which is of general interest to the industry.

Bethany and Northern Baptist Theological Seminaries (IDI)
Oak Brook, IL

Bethany and Northern Baptist Theological Seminaries Collection. The collections comprise about 10,000 items, of which some 200 titles date from the 16th century. The greatest concentration is in 18th century works. The main body represents a substantial portion of the private library of 19th century Brethren antiquarian and historian Abraham H. Cassel; second largest is Ora Huston's collection of English Bibles. Areas of emphasis include: writings of German church reformers, early Anabaptists, and 17th and 18th century Pietists; Brethren pamphlets and periodicals; tract society publications; and writings by and about Baptists.

The Center for Research Libraries (CRL)
Chicago, IL

United States Ethnic Newspaper Collection. This collection of foreign language newspapers published in the United States, primarily for the various immigrant groups, contains over 500 titles. In a significant number of instances, The Center for Research Libraries holds either the only or the longest and most complete file known. Most of these ethnic titles are held in the original format. The Center also holds the master microfilm negatives for over 85 files of ethnic newspapers.

There are 38 languages represented in The Center's collection and 30 states. The largest language group is German, followed by Italian, Polish, Swedish, and Czech, and smaller numbers for other languages. The Center maintains current subscriptions to approximately 50 ethnic titles.

Cumberland Trial Library System (IEZ)
Flora, IL

Antiques & Collectibles: "The Collector's Collection." More than 4,000 volumes of materials for the amateur collector, including books, 16mm films and 35mm slides, and serials.

DePaul University (IAC)
Chicago, IL

Charles Dickens Collection. Over 590 volumes include numerous editions of Dickens' works in the original publisher parts, first editions, first American editions, and special editions. Books about Dickens and a complete run of *The Dickensian* are also part of the collection.

Horace Collection. Contains 200 volumes of various printings and translations of the works of Quintus Horatius Flaccus, Roman lyric poet, 65–8 B.C. The collection bears imprint dates from 1554–1934 and includes many first editions.

Napoleonic Collection. The materials depict the era of Napoleon through correspondence, memoirs, and biographies of Napoleon and his family. Histories of France and Europe that reflect the social, political, and military situations of the time are included in the collection. There are 1,500 cataloged titles.

Illinois Benedictine College (ICG)
Lisle, IL

Raymond F. Neuzil Memorial Sherlock Holmes Collection. Approximately 150 pieces. Although the collection is small, its content is remarkably diverse. In addition to the Sherlock Holmes stories (in numerous editions), the collection includes juvenile editions of the stories, Holmes parodies and pastiches, works of Conan Doyle other than the Sherlock Holmes corpus, some tape recordings, and a few Japanese language

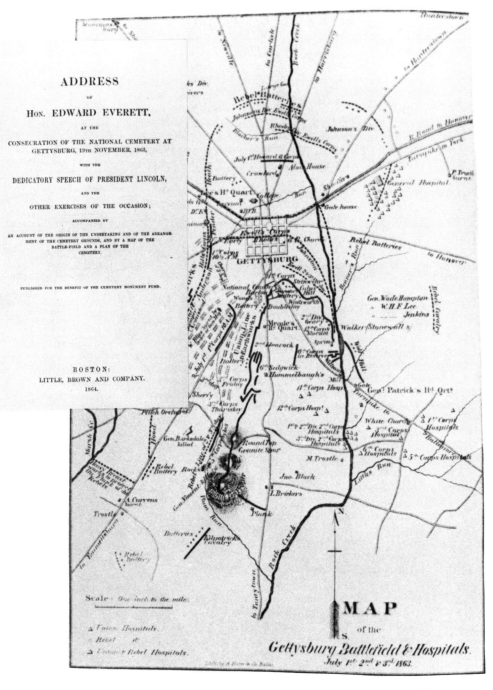

Fund-raising edition of the dedication program of the National Cemetery at Gettysburg, featuring a map of the battlefield and the address of Edward Everett. Also includes the speech of Abraham Lincoln. It was not until several years later, when Ralph Waldo Emerson singled it out, that Lincoln's Gettysburg address was generally recognized as a gem of English prose, although Everett immediately wrote to the President expressing his admiration. From the Lincoln Collection, Butler University.

works on Holmes (the latter not yet cataloged). Last, but not least, the collection includes two original volumes of *The Strand* from the early 1890s.

Illinois State University (IAI)
Normal, IL

Sage Lincoln Collection. Includes 1,300 titles and about 1,200 pamphlets. It encompasses Abraham Lincoln biographies; Lincoln memorials, eulogies, and funeral orations; Civil War materials; children's books; fiction; and books about Lincoln and his relationship to special subject areas, such as religion and slavery.

National College of Education (IGB)
Evanston, IL

Theses Collection. Contains all current theses written by master's candidates at the National College of Education either in the Foster G. McGaw Graduate School of the School of Education or in the Management and Development of Human Resources in Applied Behavioral Sciences Graduate Division of the School of Continuing Studies and the School of Arts and Sciences.

The Newberry Library (IBV)
Chicago, IL

Charles H. Kerr Publishing Co. Archives. A century of socialist and labor materials totaling more than 60,000 items, described as one of the richest collections on the history of the American Left in existence. The Archives are an invaluable resource for historians of the labor and socialist movement. Numerous editions of socialist classics, including the *Communist Manifesto* and the first complete English translation of Karl Marx's *Capital,* published by the Kerr Co., comprise part of this collection. The Archives also include many one-of-a-kind documents—letters, photographs, contracts, minutes of meetings, and manuscripts—revealing the thought and influence of such radicals as Clarence Darrow, Eugene Debs, Mother Jones, Jack London, Karl Marx, V.I. Lenin, Peter Kropotkin, Henry Demarest Lloyd, Ralph Chaplin, and Mary Marcy, all of whom were Kerr authors or contributors to Kerr periodicals.

The library also holds a choice collection of early scientific books that includes over 1,500 titles in science, medicine, technology, and pseudo-science, dating from the Renaissance through the Enlightenment. The science holdings parallel major developments in the history of science from the Middle Ages through the "scientific revolution" of the 1600s. The collection includes landmark works (many in first editions, often first impressions) by Newton, Boyle, Galileo, Descartes, and Francis Bacon, as well as works by such lesser-known authors as Gaffarel, DuLaurens, Thomas Hill, and Johann von Jessen. There is also an early two-volume reprint of the *Journal des Scavans* (Cologne, 1665–1666), the only copy in the U.S. according to *The National Union Catalog.*

The Louis Silver Collection. Includes a number of outstanding early scientific imprints. A first edition, first issue of Newton's *Principia* (1687) and the *Dialogo* of Galileo (1632), said to be the author's presentation copy, are among the holdings, as is Descartes' *Discours de la Methode* (Leyden, 1637).

John M. Wing Collection. The collection specializes in the history of printing, typography, and the book arts, emphasizing technical and graphic arts history and including incunabula and type specimen book. Leonhard Fuchs' *De Stirpium* (Basel, Isingrinius, 1542), with its elegant woodcuts of plants, is part of the collection.

Northern Illinois University (JNA)
DeKalb, IL

Byron Collection. Works by and about the English poet, including critical works and variant issues of single and collected works. Approximately 550 titles.

Colorado-Henkle Collection. Over 1,700 titles dealing with all aspects of the territory and State of Colorado. The collection includes early travel narratives, history, literature, ecology, geology, maps, and bibliography.

Drama Collections. The core is the Nisbet-Snyder Drama Collection of approximately 2,000 late 18th century and 19th century English and American plays, many of them acting copies or annotated prompt books. The collection is supplemented by the University Library Drama Collection of 212 eighteenth and early nineteenth century comic operas and acting editions of plays popular on the English stage, and 124 nineteenth century plays and 45 programs for the St. James Theatre (London) covering the period 1879–1888.

James Hanley Collection. A collection of manuscripts (some unpublished) and books by the contemporary English novelist James Hanley. Approximately 290 published titles, many variant editions.

Johannsen Collection. Copies of "dime novels" and similar American publications of the late 19th century. Also includes Johannsen's working papers and notes for his *History of the House of Beadle & Adams,* as well as papers, notes, glass plate negatives, and memorabilia from his career as a geology professor. Much of this latter material is unprocessed. Approximately 350 published titles.

Jeremy Taylor Collection. The writings of the 17th century English divine, including books referring to Taylor and influencing him as well as his own works (some editions in multiple copies). A strong and unique collection, including some manuscript material and containing approximately 400 titles.

Radical Pamphlet Collection. American publications, circa 1880–1955, by or about the radical labor movement, socialists, communists, and the radical right (including American Nazis). Material is uncataloged, but a computer index exists. Approximately 1,350 items.

Southeast Asia Collection. Cataloged holdings of the collection presently number 34,691 titles (39,374 volumes). Journal and periodical holdings (current and retrospective) number 1,368. Special strengths of this collection include the Thai, Philippine, Malaysian, Singapore, and Indonesian holdings. The Thai collection is among the largest of its kind in the U.S. Thai holdings include popular fiction, cremation volumes, official documents, and sources on the minority peoples of Thailand. Philippine holdings include numerous social science resources and documents, as well as a Philippine-American collection. The library has participated in the National Program for Acquisitions and Cataloging for Indonesia, Malaysia, Singapore, and Brunei since 1970. The University Libraries were awarded a Title II-C grant to input retrospective SEA titles into the OCLC database for improved bibliographic access.

Whitman Collection. Works by and about the American poet, including critical works and variant issues of single and collected works. Many volumes are autograph and presentation copies. Approximately 400 titles.

Southern Illinois University at Carbondale School of Law (SOL)
Carbondale, IL

Water Quality Management Plans. Comprehensive collection of Water Quality Management Plans under Sec. 208 of the Federal Water Pollution Control Act of 1972. 299 titles, 437 volumes.

University of Illinois at Urbana-Champaign (UIU)
Urbana, IL

Baskette Collection on Freedom of Expression. Ewing C. Baskette, a lawyer and librarian, owned the largest private collection of works on civil liberties and freedom of expression in the United States, comprising about 10,000 items. Within the broad definition of freedom of expression, such topics as freedom of the press, censorship, constitutional rights, religious freedom, labor union activity, well-known trials, social-ism, communism, and anarchy are represented. The collection contains many rare and unusual items, including surviving copies of books ordered to be burned and books for which their authors were executed. In addition to books, the collection also includes newspapers and periodicals, broadsides and pamphlets, manuscripts, letters, briefs, and reports of trials. Only part of the collection is currently in OCLC.

Hecht Collection. This collection consists of books and other materials relating to the American author Ben Hecht, and it includes all of his first editions, plus the first British editions and first paperbacks in most cases, as well as a selection of important reprints. Special attention is paid to variant editions, and several signed or inscribed first editions are included in the collection. Also included are first editions of works by Max-well Bodenheim, a friend and collaborator of Hecht's.

Larsen Scandinavian Collection. The 275 volumes collected by Henning Larsen consist mainly of the works of Peter Christen Asbjørnsen and Jørgen Engebretsen Moe, 19th century collectors and publishers of Norwegian folktales and legends. In addition, there are 25 Ibsen plays, of which 21 are first editions.

Mathematics. For the past two years, the Mathematics Library of the University of Illinois has input its entire collection into the OCLC database as part of a federally funded project to create a document delivery center. The project was completed on September 30, 1983. The collection supporting the University of Illinois Mathematics Document Delivery Center includes all titles that have been and will be reviewed by *Mathematical Reviews,* the major English language reviewing tool for pure and applied mathematics. The collection includes approximately 30,000 monographic and 1,500 serial titles and is particularly strong in Eastern European works, especially Russian. The collection is available through interlibrary loan or electronic mail.

Meine Collection in Folklore, Local Color, and Humor. Franklin J. Meine was a Chicago publisher and book collector particularly interested in American humor in all its forms. Formal literary satire, joke books, humorous ballads, reminiscences of fa-mous comedians, cartoons and comic almanacs, and humor magazines are all promi-nently represented in this 8,500-volume collection. It includes every important Ameri-can humorist in first editions, as well as variant editions. The **Meine Mark Twain Collection,** a collection-within-a-collection, contains about 300 first editions of Twain's books and many variant editions, including foreign translations, as well as manuscripts, memorabilia, newspaper and magazine contributions by and about Twain, and many biographical and critical volumes. Only part of the collection is currently in OCLC.

Murphy Collection. Professor Richard A. Murphy's collection of elocutionary ma-terial provides a valuable set of sources for the detailed study of a significant movement in the history of communication studies.

Nickell Collection. The Nickell Collection of 18th century English literature con-sists of original editions of Defoe, Swift, Fielding, Pope, Goldsmith, Samuel Johnson, Boswell, Addison, Smollett, and other writers of the 18th century.

Purves Collection. This collection of monographs relating to World War I includes fiction, personal narratives, and historical accounts.

Sandburg Collection. The private papers and library of Carl Sandburg include a great variety of materials. There are copies of nearly every edition of Sandburg's works, in translation as well as in English. In addition to famous works, there are many out-of-print and little-known works and some limited editions. The manuscript collection contains many of Sandburg's works, both well-known and unpublished, often in several drafts. Only part of the collection is currently in OCLC.

In addition to his own works, Sandburg owned several hundred volumes of contemporary poetry and prose, often inscribed by the author and often containing Sandburg's comments.

The materials used in the writing of the Lincoln biography are also included in the collection. There is an extensive collection of printed sources on Lincoln, as well as on the entire Civil War period.

The Sandburg collection also includes correspondence, transcriptions of Sandburg's radio broadcasts and lectures, and many newspaper clippings and articles by and about him.

Smith Collection. This collection consists of the materials assembled by Professor Richard A. Murphy for his study of the works and times of the Scottish author Alexander Smith, and it primarily contains editions of Smith's works.

H.G. Wells Archives. The papers of H.G. Wells include manuscripts, correspondence, editions of Wells' works, and miscellaneous documents. About 40 full-length books, as well as many shorter pieces, are represented in typescript or manuscript. In addition, there are 1,000 volumes of Wells' copies of his printed works. These include first editions, revisions, and translations. The letters contain general family correspondence, communications from publishers, material regarding the Fabian Society, and letters from politicians and public figures, most notably George Bernard Shaw and Joseph Conrad. Only part of the collection is currently in OCLC.

Associated Mennonite Biblical Seminaries (IME)
Elkhart, IN

The Studer Bible Collection. Well over 2,000 books and items include major divisions of English and non-English translations of the Bible, subdivisions of abridged and illustrated Bibles, Bible stories, miniatures, summaries, and concordances. There is also a library of significant books about the Bible and its preservation, printing, translation, and distribution, as well as Apocrypha and pseudo-scriptures. Unusual items in the collection include a page from the original Coverdale or Eliot Indian Bible and an 1832 copy of the Gospel of Mark and Luke in Mongolian, read perpendicularly.

Butler University (IIB)
Indianapolis, IN

American Popular Music Printed before 1901: A Collection of Sheet Music. Over 255 scores of piano music—some songs, some dance music. The collection does not circulate but single items may be photocopied. See OCLC #8081748 for a short-title list of the collection.

Catalogues: A Collection of Exhibition and Holdings Catalogues. Catalogs of famous collections, institutions, auction houses, and antiquarian dealers often become rare items in their own right. This collection of more than 185 catalogs includes many such rarities and covers a wide range of subjects. The collection does not circulate. See OCLC #13325742 for a short-title list of the collection.

William F. Charters South Seas Collection. About 2,500 volumes pertaining to the Pacific Islands and their peoples. Materials range from the earliest explorers' and circumnavigators' reports to detailed studies in anthropology, ethnology, history, botany, zoology, religion, art, socio-political structures, and music, from circa 1600 to the present. The collection is fully cataloged. About 2,000 items are currently on OCLC; the others are in the process of being converted. A partial printed catalog is available.

The largest (18″ × 22″) and smallest (2″ × 2″) Bibles in the Studer Collection, Associated Mennonite Biblical Seminaries.

The Fatherless Children of France, *a 1921 auction catalog with numerous photographs and facsimiles. From the Catalogue Collection, Butler University.*

The Dellenger Collection of Educational Materials Printed in the U.S. before 1945. More than 185 items in six categories: readers, primers, grammars, rhetoric, and music instruction; history, social sciences, business, and related subjects; mathematics; sciences and natural sciences; school history and administration; etiquette, domestic morals and virtues, home economics, and related subjects. The collection does not circulate. See OCLC #13325695 for a short-title list of the collection.

Lincoln Collection. Includes books (many of them rare and inscribed), pamphlets, campaign materials, letters, clippings, newspapers, a Lincoln manuscript, and memorabilia, mostly from the library of Charles W. Moores. All books are cataloged on OCLC. An annotated bibliography of the booklets, pamphlets, clippings, and letters was published in 1983 (OCLC #9297390). Addendum I was published in 1985.

Sibelius Collection. This collection of scores, books, recordings, photos, and memorabilia is unparalleled in the United States. It includes many compositions in hectograph and manuscript that are virtually unknown in this country. The many secondary sources provide new possibilities for Sibelius studies as well. So far, only a preliminary checklist of the scores has been made; it is cataloged as OCLC #9273684. Eventually, all scores, books, and recordings will receive individual cataloging on OCLC.

Wesenberg Collection. Twentieth century American poetry in first editions (mostly pre-1950), poetry magazines, authors' photographs, and manuscripts from the library of Alice Bidwell Wesenberg, poet and teacher (1878–1967). Many of the books are inscribed to her; some are accompanied by hitherto unpublished letters. All books are cataloged on OCLC; so are a few of the manuscripts. The magazines and the bulk of the manuscripts are being cataloged on OCLC.

Gaar Williams/Kin Hubbard Collection. Original cartoons and other drawings, books (many of them inscribed), magazines, letters, photographs, and memorabilia by both Hoosier cartoonists and humorists. A catalog of the Gaar Williams ("Abe Martin") items was published in 1981 (OCLC #9296754).

Indiana University (IUL)
Bloomington, IN

The Elisabeth Ball Collection of Children's Literature, Lilly Library. Given to the library in 1983 by the George and Frances Ball Foundation of Muncie, the collection consists of approximately 8,500 titles and a number of important manuscripts. The collection's strength lies with its British imprints and American publications, which date primarily from the late 18th and 19th centuries. The collection includes infant libraries, hornbooks, battledores, toy books, movable books, educational games, and harlequinades. Important children's publishers—John Newbery, John Harris, the Dartons, Dean and Munday, John Marshall, Frederick Warne, and others—are represented.

Jussi Bjoerling Memorial Collection. Donated by Father Jack W. Porter, founder and executive director of the Jussi Bjoerling Memorial Archive, the collection contains approximately 3,300 records and tapes of every issue of every performance recorded by Bjoerling. Also included are privately made tapes and tapes of live performances—from concerts and opera performances to radio appearances. The majority of the collection is cataloged on OCLC. *A Jussi Bjoerling Discography* (Indianapolis: Jussi Bjoerling Memorial Archive, 1982; OCLC #8481572) by Father Porter and Harald Henrysson gives a complete listing of all Bjoerling recordings.

Indiana University School of Dentistry (IUD)
Indianapolis, IN

Senior Award Essays. To meet graduation requirements, senior dental students may write a senior essay. The paper is usually around ten pages long and covers a topic relating to dentistry. A committee selects the best three papers, which are then deposited

Jussi Bjoerling, Swedish operatic tenor (Feb. 2, 1911–Sept. 9, 1960). The Jussi Bjoerling Memorial Collection at Indiana University contains records and tapes of every recorded performance by Bjoerling, whom some still consider to have been better than Domingo or Pavarotti. Photo courtesy of Willinger, Vienna.

Score of choral parts of Cantata for the University Ceremonies of 1894, for mixed chorus and orchestra, by Jean Sibelius, in the composer's hand. From the Sibelius Collection, Butler University.

permanently in the School of Dentistry Library. The collection currently consists of 127 titles. This collection is unique in that it represents original research of dental students.

Mennonite Historical Library (IMH)
Goshen, IN

Mennonite Historical Collection. Holdings in missions, conscription, colonization and migration, general and regional history, biography, genealogy (2,300 volumes, especially of Swiss and Southern German families), belles lettres, art, and cookery, either by Mennonite authors or relevant to Mennonite studies. All holdings are being entered into OCLC.

University of Evansville (IUE)
Evansville, IN

James L. Clifford Collection. Contains 828 volumes representing 642 titles consisting mainly of works by and about Samuel Johnson and James Boswell. Peripheral material includes writings of Hesther Thrale Piozzi and Fanny Burney, as well as works reflecting 18th century culture.

Grand View College (IWG)
Des Moines, IA

Danish Immigrant Archives. A collection of about 1,000 volumes of books and periodicals, plus letters and other archival material from the U.S. and Canada, mostly in Danish. Includes the DIAL (Danish Immigrant Archival Listing) project, which lists all archival holdings bearing on Danish immigration, whether housed in the U.S., Canada, or Denmark.

Grundtvig Collection. Nearly 400 volumes by and about N.F.S. Grundtvig, a Lutheran pastor, theologian, historian, educator, and writer.

Folk School Collection. Collection of books and pamphlets on the folk school movement in the U.S.

Iowa State Historical Society of Iowa (IOQ)
Iowa City, IA

Iowa History Collection. 1,377 titles including the histories of Iowa towns and counties.

Iowa State University (IWA)
Ames, IA

The American Archives of the Factual Film (AAFF). The Center for the Preservation and Study of Business, Industrial, and Educational Film was established at the Iowa State University Library in 1975. The Archives contain corporate, government-sponsored, and institutional films representing films produced from the early years of the 20th century to the present. It is the first attempt by a major institution to gather all relevant materials to document the development of the factual film in the United States. The collection is particularly strong in films dealing with agriculture, World War II and the post war era (Marshall Plan), and social behavior. As the nationwide archive and research center for the preservation and utilization of nontheatrical films, the AAFF also collects related literature and other written materials, such as filmstrips, scripts, catalogs, correspondence, and oral history tapes. Of the over 10,000 films in the collection, partial cataloging has been completed for 2,000 titles using a locally developed database. Under a 15-month grant awarded in 1981 from the U.S. Department of Education, preservation procedures and archival cataloging for input in OCLC began. Over

Frederick Starr,
Chicago, Illinois.

Ex libris for use in his collection of
books relating to Mexico and Central
America.

The subjects studied by the owner in
his Mexican researches are suggested
by the designs:

(a) Religion—past and present; the
monolithic idol and the Virgin of
Guadalupe.

(b) Archaeology; the Aztec calendar
stone.

(c) The Indian; blood (Tzendal type)
—government (Juarez)—letters (Al-
tamirano)

(d) Scenic-geology: Popocatepetl.

J. Winfred Spenceley, 1906.
Steel engraving.

Bookplate for Frederick Starr by Joseph Winfred Spenceley, from the Exlibris Collection, University of Connecticut.

400 titles are now represented in the OCLC database. Local control at a preliminary cataloging level is being secured for this collection.

E.C. Comics. Although these comic books appeared over a short period (early to mid-1950s), their brief appearance nonetheless had an impact on popular culture. Because they featured violence and horror, allegations were made that such comic books were responsible in part, for juvenile delinquency, leading in turn to an industry-wide code to prevent such publications in the future. All holdings have been cataloged. The collection contains approximately 100 issues of 18 titles.

Evolution/Creation Archive. This collection documents the ongoing controversy between evolutionists and scientific creationists. It contains books, periodicals, writings, correspondence, bibliographies, legal documents, and audio- and videotapes. The books and periodicals have been cataloged. Additions are actively solicited.

University of Northern Iowa (NIU)
Cedar Falls, IA

Modern American Fiction Collection. Approximately 3,600 volumes and growing steadily. To be included in this collection, a book must generally be: (1) a novel, (2) a first edition, and (3) written by an American who began his work in 1960 or thereafter. As these authors continue to publish and as new authors enter the field, their work is added to the collection. Significant textual forms in the collection include the American and British trade first editions, page proofs, galley proofs, movie scripts, and sound recordings. And, when the authors publish in genres other than the novel, the university collects their poetry, criticism, essays, or other nonfiction.

Benedictine College (BDC)
Atchison, KS

Feeney Collection of Hilaire Belloc. Approximately 100 volumes, containing titles both by and about Belloc.

Feeney Collection of G. K. Chesterton. Approximately 100 volumes, containing titles both by and about Chesterton.

Philosophy/Theology Collection. Approximately 38,000 volumes. Within this collection are the following "pockets" of specialization: Religious Orders of Women (in the OCLC database); Benedictina, that is, works written by/or about members, worldwide, of the Order of Saint Benedict (O.S.B.) (in the OCLC database); Monasticism; Church Fathers; and Church History (these last three subsets are in the process of retroconversion).

McPherson College (KKQ)
McPherson, KS

Church of the Brethren Archives. This collection of 5,702 items includes books, pamphlets, periodicals, and some nonprint materials by and about the Church of the Brethren and/or their people and McPherson College. McPherson College is one of four members of a consortium cataloging on OCLC using the institution symbol for Sterling College (KKQ).

University of Kansas (KKU)
Lawrence, KS

Central American Collection. The collection, acquired over the past 24 years, includes many publications resulting from recent political, social, and economic turmoil in Central America, particularly in Nicaragua and El Salvador. To date, 2,288 titles, or 2,344 volumes, have been added through a Central American Cataloging Project. An additional project began in January 1984 to add approximately 5,000 Central American titles.

William J. Griffith Collection of Central American Materials. The collection consists primarily of rare 19th century Guatemalan imprints, including 3,400 titles to be added to the OCLC database by the cataloging project which began in January 1984.

Howey Collection on the History of Economic Thought. Through a Title II-C cataloging project, 9,975 titles representing 10,226 volumes in the history of economics were added to the database. These were rare titles published between 1850 and 1930.

The Wilcox Collection of Contemporary Political Movements. A large and unique collection of U.S. extremist political literature, composed of approximately 5,000 books and pamphlets, 4,000 serial titles, and 400 audio tapes, as well as more than 50,000 pieces of ephemera. The views and ideologies of more than 7,000 left- and right-wing organizations in the U.S. are represented. The collection includes materials from the John Birch Society, the Ku Klux Klan, the American Nazi Party, the Christian Anti-Communist Crusade, Socialist Workers Party, and the Students for a Democratic Society.

University of Kansas Medical Center (KKP)
Clendening History of Medicine Library
Kansas City, KS

Logan Clendening Collection. The collection, which Clendening began as a medical student, numbered over 3,000 volumes when he founded the History of Medicine Department at the University of Kansas Medical School in 1939. It has since grown to more than 20,000 volumes, many of them first editions. Among those volumes is a rare 16th century first edition of William Harvey's treatise on blood circulation and a 200-year-old book printed in China that contains the illustration of a man performing what is known today as the Heimlich Maneuver. Vesalius' *De humani corporis fabrica* (1543) and a collection of Florence Nightingale's letters (1859) advocating nursing as a profession are also among the holdings. The Clendening History of Medicine Library is considered one of the top history of medicine libraries in the U.S.

University of Kentucky (KUK)
Lexington, KY

Applied Anthropology Documentation Collection. An archive of the written materials produced by practicing anthropologists in the course of their work: technical reports, social impact assessments, conference papers, research monographs, dissertations and theses, practicum and internship reports, bibliographies, curriculum materials, legal briefs, pamphlets, proposals, and some reprints.

W. Hugh Peal Collection. Over 5,000 titles, mainly in English and American 19th century literature.

University of Louisville, Belknap Campus (KLG)
Louisville, KY

The American Liszt Society Isidore Philipp Archive. Includes 260 cataloged titles in 361 volumes. Philipp, an eminent pianist, composer, and teacher who lived from 1863–1958, composed original piano pieces and studies and edited hundreds of others. The Louisville collection includes correspondence (letters from Liszt, Massenet, Saint-Saëns, and others), musical compositions, works edited by Philipp, pedagogical materials, and other papers documenting his career.

New Orleans Public Library (LNC)
New Orleans, LA

Louisiana Division Collection. Includes the Genealogy Section and contains books, microfilm, periodicals, Louisiana state documents, newspapers, maps, photographs, manuscripts, and other types of rare material relating to every phase of activity in the state of Louisiana, with particular emphasis on the greater New Orleans area. Special collections include the Carnival Collection of Mardi Gras material, the Louisiana Picture File, containing over 30,000 photographs, and the City Archives collection of manuscript and printed materials produced by agencies of the city.

Tulane University (LRU)
New Orleans, LA

William Ransom Hogan Jazz Archive Sheet Music Collection. More than 30,000 titles are being cataloged. Printed and manuscript music comprises sheet music, song/dance folios, orchestrations, and band music. Dates range from 1800 to the present, with an emphasis on the period from 1850–1940. Sheet music includes popular songs and piano solos; rags and ragtime songs; minstrelsy; the whole range of ante- and postbellum dance forms from the schottische through the cakewalk to the hully-gully; and coon songs. The collection of New Orleans imprints is one of the largest in existence. The collection was inaugurated by the archive's first curator and benefactor, William Russell, in the 1950s. Major donations have since been made by Al Rose, John Steiner, et al. The theater-orchestration collections include "books" of John Robichaux and Emile Tosso, both of whom were active in New Orleans' musical life from about 1890 to 1940. The cataloging project is being funded in part by the Rockefeller Foundation.

University of New Orleans (LNU)
New Orleans, LA

Ship Collection. Approximately 500 titles. Includes books on naval history, ships (general and specific), and naval architecture.

Von Der Haar Collection. Approximately 630 titles, first editions (English and foreign) of William Faulkner's novels, short stories, and poetry. The collection includes works of criticism and letters by and about Faulkner, as well as biographies and bibliographies. The collection also includes photographs and drawings.

University of Maine (MEU)
Orono, ME

Cole Collection. Includes 464 titles dealing with nautical or naval history, ships and sailing, discovery and travel, and sea life or lore. The emphasis is on the Atlantic Ocean, particularly the North Atlantic area, although many other areas are included.

Maine Collection. Works by authors who were born or resided in Maine as well as books about Maine. 4,095 titles.

Maine Juvenile Collection. 385 titles.

Rare Book Collection. 540 titles.

University of Maine at Presque Isle (UPQ)
Presque Isle, ME

Aroostook County Collection. Consists of 1,300 books and 1,400 pieces of non-print material (photos, tapes, maps, newspapers, genealogical records, etc.) on Aroostook County, Maine, or material written by Aroostook County authors.

Wood engraving bookplate by Jan Battermann of Holland, from the Exlibris Collection, University of Connecticut.

Andover Newton Theological School (BAN)
Newton Centre, MA

American Board of Commissioners for Foreign Missions Bible Collection. Includes Bibles presented to the Board by missionaries and consists of approximately 700 titles representing 98 languages.

Backus Historical Society Collection. Papers of Isaac Backus (1724–1806), Separatist and Baptist minister and historian; New England Baptist association minutes and reports of annual meetings; and 18th–19th century pamphlets.

New England Baptist Library Collection. Includes records of regional Baptist organizations and Massachusetts Baptist church records.

Clark University (CKM)
Worcester, MA

Robert Hutchings Goddard Collection. About 250 items from the rocket pioneer's personal bookshelf include classic books on rocketry, books about Goddard, and some of his favorite novels and stories, including Jules Verne's *From the Earth to the Moon.*

Archibald Hanna American Novel Collection. Over 1,200 American social novels published during the first half of the 20th century collected by Archibald Hanna, an alumnus and former curator of the Yale University Western Americana Collection.

Olive Higgins Prouty Collection. 45 titles by Ms. Prouty, Worchester native and author of *Stella Dallas,* include translations of her works into French, Spanish, Norwegian, Swedish, Portuguese, and Dutch. *Stella Dallas* was the basis of a long-running radio program, a silent film, and a feature film starring Barbara Stanwyck. Her novel *Now, Voyager* was the basis of the 1942 film with Bette Davis.

Harvard Divinity School (BHA)
Andover-Harvard Theological Library
Cambridge, MA

de Bie Library Collection. The 800 Dutch pamphlets in this collection formed part of the library of Jan Pieter de Bie (1871–1959), a Dutch church historian best known as joint editor of a multivolume biographical dictionary of Dutch Protestant clergy.

Hungarian Protestant Collection. This collection of 400 monographs and pamphlets covers the works of 19th century Hungarian Protestants.

Hymnals Collection. This collection of 19th century Protestant hymnals includes 2,500 music scores, mainly in English. There are some works in German and the Scandinavian languages.

Remonstrant Tracts Collection. This collection of 200 pamphlets consists of 17th century writings of the Dutch Protestant followers of Jacobus Arminius. The collection includes an especially large number of works by Jan Uytenbogaert (1557–1644).

Universalist Historical Society Collection. This collection of 6,000 monographs and pamphlets and 320 serials is the world's largest on the literature of the Universalist denomination, a religious group founded in England and America near the end of the 18th century. Early in the 19th century the Universalists also accepted unitarian theology and in 1961 merged with the American Unitarian Association to form the Unitarian Universalist Association. Complimentary works from the liberal religious tradition are included in this collection.

Massachusetts Institute of Technology (MYG)
Cambridge, MA

Roman Jakobson Collection on Linguistics. This collection of 9,000 monographs and 300 serial titles represents the library of this distinguished 20th century linguist. Subject strengths include: philosophy and psychology of language; morphology; syntax; semantics; Russian works on linguistics; phonetics; pathology of language, especially aphasia; comparative Indo-European linguistics; Old Church Slavonic; Slavic languages in general; comparative mythology and folklore; and Old Russian literature.

M.I.T. Publications. Some 22,500 scientific and technological publications issued by M.I.T. between 1861–1974.

Technology and Its Impact on Society. Over 13,949 titles were retrospectively converted as part of a one-year Title II-C grant retrospective conversion project. Specific subject areas: energy, computers and society, applied genetics, technology transfer, and history of technology and applied science.

Regis College Library (REG)
Weston, MA

The Father Blunt Newman Collection. Approximately 500 volumes, many first editions, by and about John Henry Cardinal Newman and over 1,500 titles relating to the Oxford Movement, Anglican Church history, and Victorian history, biography, and literature.

Suffolk University (SUF)
Boston, MA

Collection of Afro-American Literature. A cooperative venture of the Museum of Afro-American History, the Boston African American National Historic Site of the National Park Service, and Suffolk University, this collection of 3,800 titles includes poetry, drama, fiction, and nonfiction prose of all important black American writers from the 18th century to date. It contains related historical works by writers of all races, as well as periodicals. A special interest of the collection is Afro-American writers associated with New England—those who were born or who have lived and studied there. Nearly all titles are cataloged on OCLC.

Library of Michigan (EEX)
Lansing, MI

Michigan Collection. Largest collection of printed materials concerning this Great Lakes state. The collection of 20,000 volumes includes items dating from the mid-17th century, as well as recent acquisitions reflecting current social and economic issues. The collection is especially strong in local and county histories, regional fiction and poetry, and personal narratives. Retrospective conversion is currently underway.

Michigan State University Libraries (EEM)
East Lansing, MI

American Radicalism Collection. Holdings include over 12,000 monographs, serials, pamphlets, and uncataloged vertical files, with strengths in the Communist parties and organizations of the 1920–1950s, the Ku Klux Klan of the 1920–1930s, the Vietnam War/New Left period, and Third World solidarity movements in the post-Vietnam era.

Common Ground Collection. The 108 titles in this sound cassette series feature interviews with recognized experts in the fields of international relations, weapons proliferation, trade development, and other world issues. The tapes originally aired on

"Common Ground," a 30-minute weekly radio documentary series on world affairs sponsored by the Stanley Foundation of Muscatine, IA.

Conversations from Wingspread Collection. Programs in this sound cassette series feature interviews with experts and other prominent figures in many areas of public interest (1,167 titles), which includes two subseries: "Issues of Race" (29 titles) and "Conversaciones desde Wingspread" (33 titles). Conversations from Wingspread is a weekly public affairs radio broadcast series sponsored by the Johnson Foundation of Racine, WI.

The French Monarchy Collection. The collection, consisting of 9,622 titles, was originally developed by a wealthy French industrialist and was acquired by Michigan State University Libraries in 1961. It contains works spanning in subject all the years of the French Monarchy (987–1848) and includes significant resources in genealogy. Publication dates of the materials range from 1500 into the twentieth century. More than 45% of the collection is in pamphlet form, many of which are unique. Approximately 600 of the pamphlets cover the Revolutionary period; some 500 are political pamphlets published before 1700. Full level cataloging meeting national standards is being added to the OCLC database for all titles with the support of Title II-C funds. More than 75% of the titles in the collection were new to the OCLC database.

Historical Veterinary Medicine. Over 1,700 titles in veterinary medicine and related subjects, in a wide variety of languages and for most periods before 1900.

Illuminated Manuscript Facsimiles. A collection of illuminated manuscript facsimiles with holdings from the 4th century Ambrosian *Illiad* and early Vatican *Vergils* through the 16th and 17th century French and Italian Books of Hours with special strengths in the Celtic, Carolingian, and Ottonian periods of illumination.

Russell B. Nye Popular Culture Collection. Over 50,000 items, principally organized into four categories:

Comic Art Collection. This collection is the fastest growing subset of the Nye Collection. More than 1,000 monographs and nearly 1,000 serial titles in the collection have been cataloged on OCLC; about 4,000 serial titles remain to be cataloged. There is also a clipping file of comics, several dozen of which are on OCLC. Of the nearly 40,000 comic books, best represented are the superhero comics of the 1960s—over 90% of those published are in the collection. Samples and some substantial runs of other genres (war comics, funny animal comics, underground comics) are also maintained. There are also over 1,000 issues of 1940s comics and some Big Little Books.

The International Comic Art Collection. About 500 non-U.S. titles, of which about 150 have been cataloged on OCLC, are in this collection. It includes comics from Australia, Belgium, Brazil, Canada, Chile, Egypt, England, France, Germany, Greece, India, Iraq, Italy, Kuwait, Lebanon, Mexico, Netherlands, Philippines, Senegal, Spain, Sweden, and Turkey.

Popular Fiction. This subset is in turn organized in five major categories:

Detective-mystery fiction. About 3,500 novels, plus pulps representing 28 titles dating from 1920–1950, including complete runs of *The London Mystery Magazine* and *Ellery Queen's Mystery Magazine.* Also samples of the more sensational detective and crime fiction magazines from the 1930s to date.

Juvenile fiction. Emphasizes juvenile series of the 19th and 20th centuries; includes nearly 200 girls' and 300 boys' series. 19th-century "Sunday School" books and fiction and nonfiction scouting books are included.

Science fiction. Michigan State is a depository for the Science Fiction Writers of America, which contributes review copies of new books. Periodicals comprise the bulk of the collection of about 3,000 books and periodicals. Most issues date from the late 1940s to the present.

Western fiction. Over 3,000 novels (most published between 1900–1950), principally hardbound and in dust jackets, plus nearly 500 pulp magazine issues representing over 50 titles. The most important pulp runs are Street and Smith's *Western Story Magazine* and Warner Publications' *Ranch Romances.* Only a few titles are cataloged on OCLC.

Women's fiction. Over 3,000 novels and about 1,000 issues of romance, confession, and movie magazines and pulps from the 1920s–1970s, including over 2,000 Harlequin novels. Several dozen titles from late 19th-century series are included.

Popular Information. This subset of the Nye Collection includes almanacs and Blue Books. There are about 350 issues of 100 19th and 20th century almanacs and about 2,000 Little Blue Books, over 600 Big Blue Books, and numerous issues of various Haldeman-Julius magazines. The collection, totaling about 3,900 items, includes books of advice on etiquette, life and love, and how-to-succeed. There are also several hundred public school textbooks from the 19th and early 20th centuries.

Popular Performing Arts. A significant collection of primary materials relating to the tent show includes photographs, financial and other records of the Henderson Stock Co., correspondence, leaflets, handbills, and other ephemera from many of the companies playing in the upper midwest in the 1920s and 1930s, and photocopies of 250 tent show scripts.

None of the materials in the Nye Collections circulate but, when condition permits, they may be photocopied or photographed.

Monroe County Library System (EXY)
Monroe, MI

George Armstrong Custer Collection of the Monroe County Library System, Lawrence A. Frost Collection of Custerania. This burgeoning archive of materials on General Custer and the events surrounding and shaping his life includes the Frost collection, acquired in 1977. Now encompassing over 35,000 items and still expanding, the collection contains books, pamphlets, maps, manuscripts, motion pictures, slides, magazines, newspapers, paintings, photographs, sound recordings, and memorabilia. It serves as the official repository of the Little Big Horn Associates records. Monroe County Library catalogs on OCLC through the Woodlands Library Cooperative using its symbol, EXY.

Spring Arbor College (EES)
Spring Arbor, MI

Religion Collection. First edition evangelical works.

University Microfilms International (UMI)
Ann Arbor, MI

The Adler Manuscripts Collection from the Library of the Jewish Theological Seminary. 356 titles from 273 manuscripts of the 16th to 20th centuries, relating to all areas of Jewish studies. In several languages, including Hebrew, Aramaic, Latin, German, and Ladino.

Pre-1900 Canadiana. UMI has been entering Canadiana cataloging in OCLC since 1981, beginning with Unit 1 of the collection. Over 15,000 titles have been entered so far. The collection, selected and filmed by the Canadian Institute for Historical Microreproductions, includes material published in Canada, as well as material published elsewhere but written by Canadians or about Canada.

Dime Novels Collection. Escape fiction of the 19th century includes over 3,000 titles which originally appeared in various popular literature series,including cookbooks, biography, and sports books.

Early English Books, 1641–1700. This collection is selected from Donald Wing's *Short-title Catalogue*. UMI has been entering Wing cataloging in OCLC since 1981, beginning with Unit 40. Over 4,000 titles have been entered so far. Units 1–32 of the collection, consisting of 24,812 titles, have also been cataloged as a joint project by the libraries of Indiana University, University of Arizona, University of California–Riverside, University of Delaware, and University of Utah. This collection, also known as STCII, will eventually include all books printed in the British Isles and British America, as well as all English books printed in other countries during the period 1641–1700.

The History of Science Collection of the Jewish Theological Seminary. Manuscripts from the library of the Jewish Theological Seminary include 403 titles of early medical, astrological, astronomical, and other scientific works in Hebrew.

The Maimonides' Mishneh Torah Collection of the Jewish Theological Seminary. Manuscripts from the library of the Jewish Theological Seminary include 71 manuscripts of Maimonides' codification of the legal material contained in Talmudic literature.

The Adelaide Nutting Historical Nursing Collection, Teachers College, Columbia University. Over 1,200 titles, including reports, pamphlets, programs, books, and manuscripts collected by Nutting and her successors at Teachers College. Among the areas covered are the role of nurses in World War I and the career and publications of Florence Nightingale.

Presidential Election Campaign Biographies, 1824–1972. The 465 titles in this collection give both favorable and unfavorable accounts of the presidential candidates for the past 150 years.

Sahel Collection. Consists of over 900 documents and 100 doctoral dissertations, including much of the recent literature on socio-economic development in the Sahel region of Africa. The collection contains 1,041 titles.

Wayne State University (EYW)
Detroit, MI

The Eloise Ramsey Collection of Literature for Children and Young People. This collection of approximately 10,000 volumes of rare and historic literature for and about children and source materials on children's literature traces the development of children's literature from 1658 to the present. It consists mainly of 18th and 19th century American and British works and contains many rare original editions. Some famous works in foreign languages are also included. The collection is partially cataloged on OCLC.

The Leonard N. Simons Collection. A historical collection of about 1,500 items comprising monographs, rare maps, and manuscripts relating to Detroit, the state of Michigan, and the Old Northwest Territory. The monographic collection includes county histories and travel narratives of the 17th, 18th, and 19th centuries. The collection is partially cataloged on OCLC.

Bethany Lutheran Theological Seminary (MBS)
Mankato, MN

Rare Book Collection. Includes primarily Lutheran Reformation books from the 16th, 17th, and 18th centuries. Of the 923 titles in the collection, the oldest volume is the first Lutheran book of doctrine, *Loci Communes* (translated: *Basic Topics*), written by Philip Melanchthon in 1521.

College of St. Thomas (MNT)

St. Paul, MN

The Celtic Library. The library consists of approximately 4,600 titles focusing on Irish, Scottish, and Welsh history, language, literature, and folklore. About 30% of the collection is in one of the Celtic languages; the rest is in English.

The University of Mississippi (MUW)

School of Law Library
University, MS

The Stephen Gorove Special Collection in Space Law. The core of the collection is letters, memos, texts of speeches, and other materials donated by Dr. Andrew G. Haley, internationally recognized pioneer in space technology and law. In the collection at this time are 1,344 volumes, of which 297 are classified titles and 365 unclassified. The majority of the Space Law Material is classified at JX5810. The collection consists of government documents, periodicals, newsletters, and other material, including resources from NASA and the European Space Agency.

The University of Mississippi Medical Center (MRM)

Jackson, MS

The Folio Collection. Consists of oversized works which are mostly atlases of anatomy.

The Thesis Collection. Consists of 354 titles.

The Weinstein Collection. Works of fiction written by doctors.

Linda Hall Library (LHL)

Kansas City, MO

Russian and Ukrainian Science and Technology Collection. Linda Hall Library is cataloging its collection of 10,000 Russian and Ukrainian scientific/technical monographs. Mainly "sborniki," or collections of research articles, these works cover all areas of science and technology, especially applied mechanics, metallurgy, geology, chemical technology, physics, and biology. The collection's publication dates range from the late 1950s to the present; cataloging emphasis is on works from 1976 to date.

Missouri Botanical Garden (MOA)

St. Louis, MO

One of the world's most extensive collections of materials on plant systematics; plant distribution and floristic studies; plant identification; the history of botany and horticulture; herbal literature; pre-Linnean botany; biographies and bibliographies of botanists, plant explorers, and horticulturists; and other areas of botanical and horticultural science and gardening.

The St. Louis Mercantile Library Association (SLM)

St. Louis, MO

John Walker Barriger III Collection. Consists of Barriger's personal library on railroads and transportation as well as personal papers from his governmental service and railroad executive career. Contains approximately 7,100 titles.

The aloe. Plate XII from New illustration of the sexual system . . . *by Thornton, published in London in 1807. Courtesy of the Henry Francis du Pont Winterthur Museum Library: Collection of Printed Books.*

St. Louis University Law Library (SLU)
St. Louis, MO

The Smurfit Irish Law Center Collection. Founded in 1984, the Smurfit Collection contains over 500 titles (1,000 volumes) on law and law-related topics in the Republic of Ireland. Although its principal focus is the on-going acquisition of current materials, the collection does include some unique titles dating back to the 1700s. The entire collection has been cataloged on OCLC.

University of Missouri, Columbia (MUU)
Columbia, MO

De Bellis Collection. 119 titles, most in Italian, from the late Renaissance.

The Howey Collection. In the first year (1985–86) of a proposed three-year project for cataloging and preserving rare pre-1800 imprints, 5,243 volumes were cataloged. Items cataloged covered a variety of subjects in English history from Charles I to the end of Queen Anne's reign: politics, religion (primarily sermons and controversial literature), legal materials (mainly conspiracy, treason, and criminal trials; impeachment, etc.; and Parliamentary acts and proceedings). The Popish Plot and the trial and execution of Charles I, religious controversies like the Bangorian Controversy, and various scandals are among subjects covered. Interesting pamphlets include "Pro Aris et Focis," or "A Vindication of the Proceedings of the Commons on the Writs of Habeas Corpus...," in which Parliament established a precedent for the rights and liberties of all commoners in England. "An Ordinance Prohibiting Cock-Matches..." was ordered by Cromwell on March 31, 1654. This ordinance is one of the earliest regulations relating to cruelty to animals, although its primary purpose was to prevent gambling. The publication of "King William and Queen Mary Conquerors..." and the subsequent scandal surrounding its publication led to the end of English censorship of books. The collection also contains a broadside from 1649 declaring England a commonwealth following the execution of Charles I. This act ushered in an 11-year period during which there was no monarchy. It also introduced a period of intense pamphleteering by factions representing a political spectrum from royalist to democrat and a religious spectrum from Catholic to Puritan.

Thomas Moore Johnson Collection. 107 titles, predominantly works by Plato and the Platonists.

Washington University (WTU)
St. Louis, MO

Phillip Mills Arnold Semeiology Collection. This collection, numbering more than 2,000 titles, documents the early history of communications and is concerned with the study of signs and symbols. Topics covered include cryptography, codes and ciphers, artificial memory, decipherment of unknown languages, universal languages, and early developments in stenography, Braille, and various languages of the deaf and mute.

The Samuel Beckett Collection. This collection of more than 200 manuscript items includes the 28-page typescript of the radio play, *All That Fall.* There is also a collection of well over 700 printed materials by and relating to Samuel Beckett that includes signed and annotated books, limited editions, and proof copies. In a unique example of inter-institutional cooperation, Washington University and The University of Reading in England exchanged photocopies of large portions of their Beckett manuscripts for deposit in each other's repository, enabling researchers from either side of the Atlantic to have needed manuscript material available.

The Modern Literature Collection. This collection of 10,000 volumes includes exhaustive coverage of the printed work of 115 British and American authors. Proof material, variant editions, translations, periodical appearances, broadsides, and ephemera are included, as well as all editions of books by and about the authors. The collection is extensively supported with well over 100,000 manuscript pieces, including letters, notebooks, diaries, poetry worksheets, prose drafts, and other literary and personal papers. Manuscript holdings information at the collection level for 18 collections has been entered in OCLC.

University of Nebraska at Omaha (NBU)
Omaha, NE

Afghanistan Collection. The cataloged Dari and Pushto languages collection of 700 items represent a little less than half of the Afghanistan Collection of the library's special collections. The core of the Afghanistan Collection was the gift of noted Afghan studies scholar Arthur Paul.

Bergen Community College (BER)
Paramus, NJ

Passaic River Basin Study. Includes 25 titles of preliminary studies published by the U.S. Army Corps of Engineers, New York District, 1978–80.

Fairleigh Dickinson University (FDU)
Madison, NJ

Harry "A" Chesler Collection. Consists of 1,500 volumes of foreign and domestic monographs and periodicals dealing with comic art and illustration, satire, and caricature. The books support a collection of 4,000 pieces of original comic art and illustration predating 1939. Over 200 books have been cataloged on OCLC to date.

Loyd Haberly Collection. Personal library of former manager of the Gregynog Press (Wales) and the Seven Acres Press. This 750-volume collection includes examples of beautifully printed books and ephemera from contemporary private presses. Over 100 books have been cataloged on OCLC to date.

Outdoor Advertising Association of America Archive. The collection of 1,250 volumes contains books reflecting the development of the poster in most of the Western European countries and the United States. Subject matter includes posters, signage, and the outdoor advertising industry.

Health Research and Educational Trust of New Jersey (HRE)
Princeton, NJ

Hospital and Health Care Administration. The collection includes over 2,000 monographs, 250 serial titles, 700 National Library of Medicine subject files, and 200 audiovisuals.

New Jersey State Library (NJL)
Trenton, NJ

Jerseyana Collection. A local history collection of 7,630 titles in 7,853 volumes.

Wayne Public Library (WAN)
Wayne, NJ

New Jersey Historical Collection (Samuel H. Lockett Collection). Begun in 1967, this 1,700 title collection covers New Jersey history in general, with emphasis on Passaic County and the city of Wayne.

Eastern New Mexico University (IPU)

Portales, NM

Father Stanley Crocchiola New Mexico Collection. Consists of 176 titles (300 volumes) and 11 cubic feet of unpublished materials (manuscripts, notes, clippings, photographs, maps, and documents) relating chiefly to New Mexico cities and towns, land grants, historical figures, and other subjects of importance in the history of the state from territorial days to the present.

Southwest Lyric Theater and Dance Group Collection. Rare materials pertaining to theaters and touring companies in the U.S. and abroad.

Williamson Science Fiction Library. Consists of the donations of Jack Williamson and two other principal donors, Edmond Hamilton and Leigh Brackett Hamilton, primarily of published and unpublished materials in the field of science fiction. The personal papers include correspondence, manuscripts, oral history interviews, films, photographs, and memorabilia. All published works (excluding magazines) are cataloged separately in OCLC. The total holdings: 6,658 volumes, 633 magazine titles, 10,159 magazine issues, and 90 cubic feet of personal papers.

University of New Mexico (IQU)

Albuquerque, NM

Archives of the Indies Collection. Over 600 bound volumes of photostat manuscript material. Originals are located in Archive of the Indies, Seville, Spain.

Batchelder-McPharlin Puppetry Collection. A composite collection of books, personal correspondence, music, art, and realia relating to all phases of puppetry including technical, educational, and therapeutic uses. There are some 2,200 items, including 123 unpublished puppet play manuscripts, 132 printed plays, 104 books on puppetry in Russian, 19 international periodicals, and 163 items of realia. Historical and international in scope, it covers Europe, Indonesia, East Asia, the Americas, and has a special emphasis on Eastern Europe and Russia.

Anita Osuna Carr Bicultural/Bilingual Collection. This collection of children's literature and classroom materials housed in the Tireman Learning Materials Library includes hard-to-find editions in Spanish, Spanish and English, and Native American languages and English. The collection numbers over 2,250 titles, the great majority of them in Spanish. About 125 titles are in Navajo or Navajo and English, and there are smaller groups in other Native American languages, Spanish and English, Portuguese, Vietnamese, and Laotian.

Gigante Collection. Comprises 733 titles, 463 scores, 135 miniature scores, 403 piano scores, 25,811 parts of orchestral music of the major classical composers. The collection is unique because of the original bow marking annotations on the scores by many of the world's leading conductors.

Helm Collection. A collection of music scores comprising 400 titles of 18th and 19th century French opera and art songs. Some of the scores are first editions, many are autographed, and there is some correspondence associated with the collection.

Van de Velde Collection. 8,700 monographs, 93 groups of manuscript material, hundreds of broadsides, pamphlets, and handbills dealing with Mexican and Meso-American ethnohistory economics, linguistics, art, and architecture from the 17th–20th centuries.

Alfred University (YAH)

Alfred, NY

Waid Collection. Consists of about 700 titles (over 1,000 items) published in Germany, mostly in the 1930s and 1940s. Donated by H. Warner Waid, an alumnus, the

From the 1618 edition of the first work of veterinary anatomy based on Vesalian prin-ciples, Carlo Ruini's Anatomia del Cavallo, Infermita, et Svoi Rimedii. *From the Loren Carlson Health Sciences Library, University of California, Davis.*

books are largely the sort which would have been found in the average German home and are a valuable picture of the growth and dominance of Nazism in Germany. Recently added are periodicals and monographs about the occupation and rehabilitation of Germany collected from Allied and American High Commissions and State Department branches by Mr. Waid, who was Editor-in-Chief of the official U.S. Army of Occupation *Information Bulletin*. A guide to the collection is in process.

Hofstra University (ZIH)
Hempstead, NY

Weingrow Collection of Avant-Garde Art and Literature. Includes approximately 3,300 books, periodicals, art catalogs, and original prints that document the activity of the major literary and artistic movements of the 19th century: Dadaism, Surrealism, Expressionism, Cubism, Futurism, Nuclear Art, Pop Art, and others. The collection, emphasizing foundation documents pertaining to these movements, also includes primary and secondary works of related movements of the late 19th century, such as German Romanticism, Art Nouveau, and Symbolism.

Mercy College (VZE)
Dobbs Ferry, NY

Millbrook Hunt Collection of Equestrian Arts. Covers the entire range of the subject, including horse care and health, riding skills, as well as the techniques and lore of the hunt. There are 517 monographic titles and 12 periodical titles in the collection.

Nazareth College of Rochester (XNC)
Rochester, NY

Baring Collection. Principally first editions of the works of Maurice Baring, friend of G.K. Chesterton and Hilaire Belloc, but among the 75 items are several biographies. Baring was noted and admired for his interest in pre-revolutionary Russia; the collection includes his *The Russian People* (1911).

Byrne Collection. Some 198 volumes from the collection of Msgr. Edward J. Byrne reflect his life-long interest in the history of Auburn (NY) and adjacent regions; 109 of the items are Auburn imprints, almost entirely of the period 1840–1860 (some 17% of all titles published in Auburn in that period). The collection enlarges the resources available to scholarship in regional American bibliography and the study of readership in America during the mid-19th century.

Chesterton Collection. Some 225 items, plus microfilm, include separately published trade editions of works by and about G.K. Chesterton. British first editions of the *G.K. Chesterton Calendar* (1916), *Return of Don Quixote* (1927), and the American first edition of *Utopia of Usurers* (1917) are among the titles.

Hendrick Papers. Correspondence of the first American bishop of Cebu in the Philippine Islands, almost all from 1903–1909. The 273 pieces shed light on the problems of religion in a society wracked by revolution and devastated by protracted military operations and illuminate the culture-shock resulting when a wholly new set of goals is adopted by a society.

Sitwell Collection. A growing collection of over 170 first and other significant editions of works by and about Dame Edith, Sir Osbert, and Sacheverell Sitwell.

New York Botanical Garden (VXG)
Bronx, NY

One of the world's most extensive collections of materials on plant systematics; plant distribution and floristic studies; plant identification; the history of botany and horticulture; herbal literature; pre-Linnean botany; biographies and bibliographies of botanists, plant explorers, and horticulturists; and other areas of botanical and horticultural science and gardening.

Saint Bonaventure University (VYS)
Saint Bonaventure, NY

Franciscan Institute Collection. Approximately 15,000 books, 5,000 periodicals, 250 incunabula, 120 manuscripts, and 3,000 rare books published between 1501 and 1825, with emphasis on the life of St. Francis of Assisi and the Franciscan movement in general and also on the Spanish conquest of the New World.

St. Lawrence University (XLM)
Canton, NY

Irving Bacheller Papers. Mr. Bacheller was a best-selling author and lecturer at the turn of the century. This collection of about 400 items (4 ft.) contains business and personal letters, photographs, newspaper clippings, and drafts of several works, some unpublished.

Alvah Beach Letters. About 100 letters written by Alvah and Enos Beach of Russell, NY, while they were in the Union Army during the Civil War. Includes two daguerreotypes of Alvah Beach and materials relating to David Robinson, brother-in-law of the Beach brothers.

Joseph Child Papers. Records of the land business of James Moon of Middletown, PA, which he sold through his relatives and agents, Daniel, Joseph, and Moses Child. Included in the nearly 100 items are maps and descriptions of the lots belonging to Moon, accounts of the payments by buyers, and correspondence between Moon and the Childs. There are also references to the Quaker affairs of the area and information on the settlement of Philadelphia, NY.

Ulysses Sumner Milburn Collection of Hawthorniana. Included in the nearly 1,200 items that make up this collection are 39 letters written by Nathaniel Hawthorne and a number of letters written by members of the Hawthorne family and friends. Also included are manuscripts by Hawthorne, the most numerous among these are documents related to his business and financial affairs.

State University of New York, Agricultural and Technical College at Alfred (ZAM)
Alfred, NY

Western New York Historical Collection. This collection of some 2,256 volumes, (1,495 titles) includes material covering the area from Syracuse on to the west, with a concentration on Allegany and adjacent counties. (A few of the items are on long-term loan from the Alfred Historical Society.) In addition to local history, the collection includes genealogical material and some old works relating to agriculture and technology, of value because of the background of the college. Oral histories and other audiovisual items, as well as collections of transactions of various local and community organizations, personal papers, letters and diaries, and extensive local weather and cemetery records are included.

State University of New York, College at Buffalo (YBM)
Buffalo, NY

The Creative Studies Collection. This interdisciplinary collection consists of approximately 3,000 monographs, 2,000 dissertations, and 50 audiovisual items. The emphases of the collection are in the psychology of creativity and instruction in creative thinking.

State University of New York, College of Arts and Sciences at Geneseo (YGM)
Geneseo, NY

Carl F. Schmidt Collection on Historical Architecture. Located in the Milne Library, the collection contains notes, sketches, slides, photos, manuscripts, measured drawings, and scrapbooks covering architecture in western New York State.

Wadsworth Family Papers, 1789–1952. Also housed in the Milne Library, this collection contains some 55,000 items from business and family correspondence, account books, maps, deeds, leases, and business records of the Wadsworth family, early landowners in the Genesee region of western New York. Prominent persons represented in the correspondence include Theodore Roosevelt and Henry Cabot Lodge.

State University of New York, College at Fredonia (XFM)
Fredonia, NY

Holland Land Company Archives. Well over 200 reels of microfilm and other publications—detailed correspondence, inventories, descriptions, land records, surveys, and maps—associated with the company's business operations and land holdings in New York and Pennsylvania, 1789–1869. Most of the microfilms contain copies of the archival materials owned by the Municipal Archives of Amsterdam (The Netherlands). Information pertaining to other sections of the U.S., including specific cities such as Philadelphia, is included as part of the company's information gathering.

Music Collection. Contains 32,000 scores and about 15,000 sound recordings.

Western New York Local History Collection. Approximately 550 cubic feet of material, principally devoted to manuscripts and published works in all formats relating to Chautauqua and Cattaraugus counties and the College. Of special interest are materials relating to the Holland Land Company, the Chautauqua Institution, and the Grace Richmond papers.

Stefan Zweig Collection. The Reed Library houses over 8,500 of Zweig's letters, including the complete correspondence between Stefan Zweig and his wife, Friderike, as well as more than 350 volumes of Zweig's published works in their various editions, and works written about Zweig. The collection contains a wealth of information related to 20th century European humanism.

State University of New York, College at Oneonta (ZBM)
Oneonta, NY

Children's Collection. This collection of 14,000 titles, from preschool through 9th grade, was built from the campus school collection. Old as well as new titles are included.

Late 19th & Early 20th Century Popular Fiction Collection. Includes 2,200 English language novels and short stories written before 1920. The collection is limited to popular literature and excludes works of literary significance.

New York State Verse Collection. A collection of 200 books, pamphlets, broadsides, and a few manuscripts written before 1920 by New Yorkers or inspired by New York subjects. It excludes the works of poets who have achieved literary recognition.

State University of New York, State College of Optometry (VXP)
New York, NY

The Harold Kohn Vision Science Library. Approximately 12,000 titles and 22,000 volumes of books and audiovisual materials devoted to optometry and vision-related subjects that impinge on optometry.

State University of New York, University at Buffalo (BUF)
Buffalo, NY

Morris L. Cohen Rare Book Collection of the Charles B. Sears Law Library.
This collection of some 1,000 volumes contains 16th- and 17th-century British legal
works (yearbooks, reports, institutes, etc.) and 18th- and 19th-century American legal
works (reports, compendia of state and federal laws, etc.). Items with main entries beginning with letters A–F (and some Gs) have been entered into the OCLC database. The
entire collection is included in the *Checklist of Rare Materials in the Charles B. Sears
Law Library,* published in 1981 (OCLC #7900832).

History of Medicine Collection. This collection, established in 1972 in the University's Health Sciences Library, consists of some 10,500 volumes, plus manuscripts, yearbooks, and medical instruments. It focuses on 19th century works with emphasis on
obstetrics and gynecology, surgery, dentistry, psychology, and pharmacology. It includes
the library holdings of the Buffalo Medical College (founded 1846) and of the Schools
of Pharmacy (established 1886) and Dentistry (established 1892). The entire collection,
aside from the instruments, has been entered into the OCLC database.

Polish Room Collection. The collection consists of over 7,000 items—books, serials,
letters, diaries, manuscripts, and photographs, as well as some films and slides—ranging
from 17th-century royal documents to recently published materials. The collection focuses on Poland's arts and history, with the primary function of preserving and trans-
mitting the Polish cultural heritage. It is particularly strong in monumental reference
works. Most material is in Polish, but the collection does contain material in English
and other languages that relates to Poland or to Poles in the U.S. and other countries.
  The nucleus of the collection was given to the University Libraries by the Polish Arts
Club of Buffalo in 1955. All printed materials added to the collection since 1974 have
been entered into the OCLC database. As of 1986 about 50% of the collection had been
entered, with the balance to be added through retrospective conversion.
  In 1983 the University Libraries published a two-volume author-title and subject catalog (OCLC #9999991) of the collection as it existed at the end of 1982.

20th Century Poetry in English Collection. In addition to the first and variant
editions of every major and a large number of minor poets from the U.S., Great Britain, Canada, Australia, and New Zealand, this collection contains critical and attendant
material relating to those poets and their works. Special strengths are the large manuscript and book collections of James Joyce, Robert Graves, and William Carlos Williams.
The collection consists of some 88,000 titles, 75,000 letters, and 100,000 manuscripts.
Included are some 6,000 broadsides, 3,500 little magazine titles (of which 1,200 are
current subscriptions), and a 7,000-volume collection of literary anthologies. A catalog
of current holdings of the periodicals is updated and printed bi-monthly. About 55,000
titles have been entered in the OCLC database.

Syracuse University (SYB)
Syracuse, NY

The Ranke Collection. This is the library of the German historian Leopold von Ranke
(1795–1886), called the father of modern history, and was acquired after his death. It
contains approximately 6,500 monographic titles, 4,000 pamphlets, 400 manuscripts,
approximately 300 serial titles, and 300 maps, the cataloging of which has not yet begun. Among the holdings are Mercator's *Atlas Minor,* which includes some of the oldest printed maps of the New World, and Copernicus' *De Revolutionibus Orbium Coe-
lestium* (Concerning the Revolving of Heavenly Bodies). The collection is strongest in
European history, biography, church history, and related fields. Most of the books are
in German, Latin, French, Italian, or English; chronologically, the printed materials range
from 1485–1886.

A portrait of King Charles I from the Eikon Basi-like, *London 1648, Madan no. 3, first issue. From the 17th Century Theology and Politics Collection, University of Rochester.*

One of the Horatio Alger "dime novels" published in the early 1900s by Street & Smith of New York. From the Dime Novels Collection, University of Rochester.

University of Rochester (RRR)
Rochester, NY

Among the nearly 75,000 volumes in the Department of Rare Books and Special Collections are these collections:

Contemporary American Literature. In-depth collections of contemporary novelists and poets, including John Gardner, William Heyen, Galway Kinnell, and Frederick Exley.

Dime Novels. Representative collection of more than 10,000 American dime novels, ca. 1860–1915. Includes Nick Carter, Horatio Alger, Buffalo Bill, Frank Merriwell, and Pluck and Luck.

The Filmed Book Collection. Approximately 1,000 first edition volumes, mostly books that have been made into films.

Mary Faulk Markiewicz Collection of Children's Books. Approximately 1,000 children's books, mostly 19th-century works of fiction, poetry, and nonfiction; many are upstate New York imprints.

The Sydney Ross Collection of John Ruskin. More than 400 volumes of first and early editions by and about Ruskin.

17th-Century Theology and Politics. Approximately 300 volumes on late 17th-century English religious-political controversy, with emphasis on William Sherlock. A subset, the *Eikon Basilike* collection, holds about 25 editions of this work purported to be King Charles I's meditations.

Slavery Source Materials/Microcard Editions. Approximately 500 books and pamphlets written before the Civil War by and about Blacks, from the Negro Collection of the Fisk University Library.

Southern Newspapers. Approximately 1,000 reels of mainly Savannah 19th-century newspapers.

The University of North Carolina at Chapel Hill (NOC)
Chapel Hill, NC

Bowman Gray Collection of World Wars I & II. The Gray Collection includes approximately 16,000 items from 20 countries (posters, photographs, portraits, and other war-related graphic items), the majority of which were produced during World War I.

Hanes Collection of Estiennes. The Rare Book Collection of the university houses this special collection, which was acquired through the support of the Hanes Foundation for the Study of the Origin and Development of the Book. There are 300 titles in the collection, which consists of 16th and 17th century books from the publishing houses of the Estienne family, the foremost group of scholar-printers of the period. They were leading scholars in editing texts, compiling dictionaries, designing type, and publishing classical, medical, and religious works. Some of the more important works include Robert Estienne's monumental *Latinae Linguae Thesaurus* (1543), a work of Latin lexicography that is still the most complete work of its kind, and Henri Estienne's first complete edition of Plato (1578), whose pagination provided the system of reference to the text of Plato that is still in use.

The Health Sciences Library has a special collection of 2,000 rare books in medicine, nursing, pharmacy, epidemiology, and dentistry.

The North Carolina Spanish Theater Collection. One of the most complete sources anywhere for the study of Spanish drama and opera, the collection consists of some 26,000 separately published plays and libretti in Castilian and Catalan, spanning the late 17th to the mid-20th centuries. Some 2,000 of the earlier plays are in the *comedia suelta* format. A large part of the collection (over 21,000 records) is entered into the OCLC database.

Wake Forest University (NBG)
Bowman Gray School of Medicine
Winston-Salem, NC

The John and William Hunter Collection. 53 titles comprise this growing collection of primary and secondary works by and about 18th century Scottish physicians and brothers, John (1728–1793) and William (1718–1783) Hunter. John Hunter's *Observations on certain parts of the animal oeconomy* (1786) is included.

The Locked Case Collection. The core of this collection is from the two-year medical program at Wake Forest College (1906–1940). Expanded over the years, the collection, which numbers over 750 titles, allows the medical school community access to the scientific and popular development of medicine through the ages. Recent gifts include editions of Malpighi's *Opera omnia* (1687), Cullen's *First Lines of the Practice of Physic* (1790), and Valverde's *Anatome corporis humani* (1607).

Lawrence C. McHenry, Jr., M.D. Collection in the History of Medicine and Neurology. Over 1,200 titles from Dr. McHenry's private collection represent a lifetime of interest and research in the history of medicine and neurology. Dr. McHenry (1929–1985) revised and edited Garrison's *History of Neurology* in 1969. The collection includes material on the development of American neurology, with books by and about Francis X. Dercum, William Hammond, and the Philadelphia Hospital for Orthopedic and Nervous Diseases. The book collection, cataloged on OCLC, is companion to a collection of personal papers, not completely processed, that deals with Dr. McHenry's clinical and historical research, as well as his personal life.

Suzanne Meads Art in Medicine Collection. Over 150 titles of primary and secondary works concerning the relationship of art and medicine, with an overview of the impact art and medicine have on each other and society. Selected reprint editions as well as nonbook material complement the core collection.

North Dakota State University (TRI)
Fargo, ND

The Germans from Russia Heritage Collection. Consists of about 300 volumes, all of which are on OCLC. English and German language materials document the migration of Germans to Russia and their life there, particularly in the Black Sea and Bessarabia regions.

North Dakota History Collection. About 3,000 books devoted to the history of North Dakota. The collection is housed in the North Dakota Institute for Regional Studies, which also administers a manuscript collection, historic photographs, and the university archives. Over 50% of the collection is on OCLC.

The Cleveland Health-Sciences Library of the Cleveland Medical Library Association and Case Western Reserve University (CHS)
Cleveland, OH

The Robert M. Stecher Collection of Charles Darwin Books and Manuscripts. One of the outstanding resources in the United States for the study of Charles Darwin. Included are such rarities as the first edition of *The Origin of Species,* extracts from letters addressed to Professor Henslow (1835) (OCLC #1151368), Thomas Malthus' *Principles of Population* (1798), and Charles Lyell's *Principles of Geology* (1830 –1833).

Over 175 manuscript letters by Darwin, his family, and contemporaries are an invaluable part of the collection.

In addition to the books and manuscripts, the collection contains articles, reviews, and ephemera (both 19th and 20th century) relating to Darwin and Darwinism. Included are pictures, caricatures, obituaries, original reviews and reactions to the *Origin,* and correspondence with famous Darwinian scholars.

Cleveland Public Library (CLE)
Cleveland, OH

The John G. White Collection of Folklore, Orientalia, and Chess. The White Collection, with over 134,000 volumes and more than 7,000 languages and dialects represented, originated as the personal library of John Griswold White, a noted Cleveland attorney. Three subject areas are broadly defined: the orientalia classification includes books in both Asian and Western languages and books on Asia from the Near East to Easter Island; folklore includes folk tales and medieval romances, chapbooks, and gypsy lore; chess includes material on checkers as well as chess and rich collections of works such as Castiglione's *The Courtier* and Rabelais' *Gargantua and Pantagruel* (which make significant references to chess although they are not primarily concerned with the Royal Game).

Cleveland State University (CSU)
Cleveland, OH

Hazel Collister Hutchison Contemporary Poetry Collection. The collection of approximately 700 monographic titles and approximately 200 literary and little magazine titles (in broken sets) emphasizes British and American poetry written or published in English since 1945. Translations are included if they meet the date scope.

Defiance College (DEF)
Defiance, OH

The Afro-American Culture Collection. A collection of approximately 1,150 volumes by and about Blacks.

The Eisenhower Collection. A collection of approximately 250 volumes both by and about President Dwight D. Eisenhower.

Indian Wars Collection of Northwestern Ohio. Consists of approximately 250 volumes that deal with General Anthony Wayne's campaign and other Indian wars of the period 1780–1815.

Heidelberg College (HEI)
Tiffin, OH

Besse Collection. 5,146 titles, 6,920 volumes of published correspondence, chiefly English and American, of which about 750 are rare or difficult to find items.

Kent State University (KSU)
Kent, OH

The James Broughton Papers. In addition to the manuscripts of Broughton's major books, there are unpublished journals and novels as well as correspondence with Helen Adam, Robert Creeley, Robert Duncan, Madeline Gleason, Willard Maas, Frank O'Hara, Eve Triem, and Jonathan Williams.

Children's Literature Collection. In 1977 Kent acquired the archives of Akron's Saalfield Publishing Co., one of the world's leading publishers of children's books. The company had exclusive literary rights to Shirley Temple and also published the Boy Scout and Campfire Girl series, dot books, sewing cards, and activity boxes, most of which are preserved in mint condition.

Another important children's literature collection is devoted to Alice in Wonderland and includes some 50 editions of the Lewis Carroll classic—some volumes with the bookplate of Morris L. Parrish, a leading Alice collector.

More high spots of the collection are Louisa May Alcott's *Little Women* (1868), Randolph Caldecott's *Picture Books* (1878–1885) with an original drawing, Mark Twain's *Huckleberry Finn* (1885), a complete set of Kate Greenaway's *Almanacks* (1883–1897), Kate Douglas Wiggin's *Rebecca of Sunnybrook Farm* (1903), the Big Little Book of *Little Orphan Annie* (1928) and the first issue of the *Superman* comic book (1939). There is also a collection of published children's writing and books about teaching children to write.

Contemporary Poetry Collection. 3,500 items by and about writers of "the Beat Generation." Of the quarter of a million volumes from the Gilman Bookstore in Crompond, N.Y. came key titles by Conrad Aiken, W.H. Auden, Countee Cullen, Paul Laurence Dunbar, Kenneth Patchen, Gertrude Stein, and Oscar Wilde and comprehensive collections of William Carlos Williams and Robert Frost.

Dramatic Literature and the Performing Arts Collections. The Erich T. Griebling Drama Collection was established in 1970 with books from the library of the longtime English professor. Among the playwrights collected are Edward Albee, Samuel Beckett, Arthur Miller, Eugene O'Neill, Harold Pinter, George Bernard Shaw, David Storey, Thornton Wilder, and Tennessee Williams. A collection of research material assembled by **G. Harry Wright** (1901–1964) about showboats in general and Kent State's involvement with the Majestic in particular was donated by the veteran theater professor's widow in 1978. A regional theater collection of programs, posters, and press releases from such companies as the Goodman Theater (Chicago), and the Guthrie Theater (Minneapolis) is highlighted by a major concentration of materials from Cincinnati's Playhouse in the Park, including annotated production books.

The Feiss Collection. Among the Feiss books are Ariosto's *Orlando Furioso* (1550), the Venerable Bede's *History of the Church of Englande* (1565), Holinshed's *Chronicles* (1587), Sir Thomas Browne's *Hydriotaphia* (1658), the Kelmscott Press edition of William Morris' *The Defense of Guenevere* (1892) and the Doves Press edition of Emerson's *Essays* (1906).

Fiction Collection. The fiction collection begins with the beginnings of fiction. Early British titles include Henry Fielding's *Tom Jones* (1749) and Tobias Smollett's *Peregrine Pickle* (1751). Holdings of America's first novelist Charles Brockden Brown form the basis of the definitive edition of Brown. Of special interest is Daniel Edwards Kennedy's unpublished manuscript biography of Brown.

Among the prominent contemporary author collections are a comprehensive gathering of all William Faulkner published during his lifetime, the John O'Hara collection of his biographer-bibliographer Matthew J. Bruccoli, and a Joseph Conrad collection.

A major detective fiction collection includes the writings of Raymond Chandler and Georges Simenon.

Other contemporary novelists collected in depth are Sherwood Anderson, Djuna Barnes, Kay Boyle, Thomas Burke, Gabriel Fielding, F. Scott Fitzgerald, John Galsworthy, Ernest Hemingway, Henry James, James Joyce, D. H. Lawrence, Paul Metcalf, Anais Nin, James Stephens, Kurt Vonnegut, Jr., H. G. Wells, Virginia Woolf and Richard Wright.

Curiosities in the collection include a parcel of science fiction paperbacks and a collection of Armed Services Editions of World War II.

The Virginia Glenn Memorial Collection of Readings in Human Potential. The collection includes works in the fields of parapsychology, psychedelic drugs, dreams, and the occult.

History Collections. Notable volumes in the collection are Martin Luther's *Kirchen Poltilla Das Ist* (1555), Cotton Mather's *Magnalia Christi Americana* (1702), Jonathan Carver's *Travels Through the Interior Parts of North America* (1779), James Bruce's

The hogfish. Plate 15 from Volume II of
Catesby's Natural History. Courtesy of the
Henry Francis du Pont Winterthur Museum
Library: Collection of Printed Books.

Child's bookplate etching by John William
Jameson, from the Exlibris Collection, University of Connecticut.

Travels to Discover the Sources of the Nile (1790), Tench Coxe's *A View of the United States of America* (1794), Allen F. Gardiner's *Narrative of a Journey to the Zoolu Country in South Africa* (1836), Paul Allen's *History of the Expedition Under the Command of Captains Lewis and Clark to the Sources of the Missouri* (1814), Henry Trumbull's *History of the Discovery of America* (1828), Alexis de Tocqueville's *Democracy in America* (1838), J. C. Fremont's *Report of the Exploring Expedition to the Rocky Mountains* (1845), and the second book appearance of Abraham Lincoln's *Gettysburg Address* (1863). Historical manuscripts include a 1765 lottery ticket signed by John Hancock, an 1813 Pennsylvania German fraktur by the Smoke Church artist, notebooks of 19th century American painter Miner K. Kellogg and the diaries of Ona Simaite, the Lithuanian librarian condemned to death by the Nazis for helping Jews escape.

History of Printing and Small Presses Collection. The oldest printed book in the library is St. Hieronymous' *Aureola ex floribus contexta* (1470–72) published by Sensenschmidt in Nuremberg. It is one of 13 incunables housed in the collection. Key books in the history of printing are Hardouyn's *Book of Hours* (1528), Plantin's printing of Aesop's *Fables* (1574), Benjamin Franklin's printing of *An Extract from a Treatise of William Law* (1760), the Baskerville Bible (1763), the Isaiah Thomas printing of Bancroft's *Essay on the Life of George Washington* (1807), the Chiswick Press edition of Walton's *The Complete Angler* (1826), the Kelmscott *Chaucer* (1896), and Dard Hunter's *Before Life Began* (1941) designed by Bruce Rogers for the Rowfant Club.

Other imprints include the Alternative Press of Detroit, Arkham House, Auerhahn Press, Black Sparrow Press, Broadside Press of Detroit, Coach House Press, Divers Press, Elizabeth Press, Grabhorn Press, the Jargon Society, North Atlantic Books, Origin Press, Perishable Press, Stone & Kimball, and Trianon Press.

In the 1950s the library acquired from Elisabeth Clark Tyler Miller of Cleveland a collection of over 30,000 bookplates covering every period of bookplate design in the U.S., Great Britain, and Europe. These, along with books and periodicals about bookplates, are housed in Special Collections.

There are also small but select collections of fore-edge paintings and early textbooks, including three dozen McGuffey readers.

The George C. Lamb Memorial Collection of Cryptography. This collection on cryptography was initiated in 1970 in memory of George Chester Lamb (1906–1939), a president of the National Puzzler's League and the first editor of *The Cryptogram*. Among the original volumes were Helen Fouche Gaines' *Elementary Cryptanalysis* (1939) inscribed by Gelett Burgess and a signed copy of Luigi Sacco's *Manuale di Crittografia* (1947). The following year the American Cryptogram Association added its library to the collection.

Mariana Collection. In 1951 Ray Baker Harris presented his collection of books, scrapbooks, and other material relating to Queen Marie of Romania to Kent. The collection was the result of Harris' long friendship with Queen Marie and contains inscribed copies of many of her books, photographs of the royal family, and general works on Romania.

The James Robert Parish Reference Library. Few writers on the movies have been as prolific as James Robert Parish, who counts among his 40 books *The MGM Stock Company* (1973), *The Elvis Presley Scrapbook* (1975), and *The Leading Ladies* (1977). His personal film reference library of some 1,000 volumes and numerous periodicals forms the basis of the Parish Collection, to which he has added manuscripts, correspondence, and clipping files.

Science. Perhaps the rarest item in this collection is a copy of Howard Jones' *Illustrations of the Nests and Eggs of Birds of Ohio* (1879–1886). Issued in parts, the work contains 68 hand-colored plates which have been called the finest work since Audubon. Only 90 copies were produced and four were imperfect or destroyed.

A small collection of herbals contains works by Rembert Dodoen (Antwerp, 1616), John Gerarde (London, 1633), Nehamiah Grew (London, 1682), William Salmon (Lon-

The Wright Brothers Collection, Wright State University.

Diamond-shaped bookplate with monogram of the Tsarina Alexandra, wife of Nicholas II and last empress of Russia. The plate appears in the Romanov's personal library copy of the five-volume works of Grotius, published in Russian in St. Petersburg in 1898. From Miami University Library, Oxford, Ohio.

don, 1710), and John Hill (London, 1756). The collection also includes 43 diaries of amateur naturalist George Jason Streator (1846–1925), which detail his studies of land and fresh-water shells. A fingernail clam—*Pisidium streatori*—was named in his honor.

Among highlights in the collection are Erasmus Darwin's *Zoonomia* (1794–1796), John Abbot and James Edward Smith's *Natural History of the Lepidopterous Insects of Georgia* (1797), William Maclure's *Observations on the Geology of the United States* (1817), Robert D. Foster's *The North American Indian Doctor* (1838), W. W. Mather's *First Annual Report on the Geological Survey of the State of Ohio* (1838), Edgar Allan Poe's *The Conchologist* (1839), Charles Darwin's *On the Origin of Species* (1859), Louis Agassiz's *Geological Sketches* (1866), H.G. Wells' *Textbook of Biology* (1893), and the patron edition of William Leon Dawson's *The Birds of California* (1923).

The Ulizio Collection. B. George Ulizio (1889–1969) was one of President Roosevelt's "dollar-a-year men" during the Depression. He collected primarily British and American literature. A highlight of his 1,500-volume collection is what is believed to be one of the largest collections of copyright deposit copies outside the Library of Congress, including Emerson's *Nature* (1836), Bret Harte's *The Luck of Roaring Camp* (1870), and Lafcadio Hearn's *Some Chinese Ghosts* (1887). Other significant books in the collection are Dickens' *Nicholas Nickleby* (1838–39) in parts, the dedication copy of Poe's *Tales of the Grotesque and Arabesque* (1840), Stephen Crane's *Maggie* (1893), and the first publication of the Hogarth Press, Leonard and Virginia Woolf's *Two Stories* (1917).

The William E. Warner Collection. Warner (1897–1971) was a pioneer in technology education and founder of Epsilon Pi Tau, the industrial arts honorary. His 900 volume library, plus 15 boxes of correspondence and manuscripts, includes a signed copy of William Morris' *Hopes and Fears for Art* (1882), the Kelmscott Press edition of *Stories of the Emperor Coustans* (1894), and Dard Hunter's *Papermaking Through Eighteen Centuries* (1930).

Other collections and the number of volumes included are:

Holocaust Literature. 250 volumes.

Law Collection. 3,000 volumes.

Ohioana Collection. 2,160 volumes.

Parapsychology Collection. 450 volumes.

Science Fiction Collection. 930 volumes.

Miami University (MIA)
Oxford, OH

Louise Bogan Collection. The working library of this American poet and critic contains some 1,700 volumes, many annotated by her, including inscribed review copies.

Botanic Medicine Collection. Emphasizing 19th-century American works, this group of 350 titles includes herbals from the 17th and 18th centuries.

William Dean Howells Collection. 800 volumes and 120 manuscript items compose a collection of works by and about the Ohio author.

King Collection of Juvenile Literature. Some 10,000 items illustrate the development of children's literature from the 16th century to date. The collection of periodicals, chapbooks, movable and toy books, and miniature books is complemented by an extensive reference collection.

A.W. Kuchler Vegetation Map Collection. The entire collection of maps described in *The International Bibliography of Vegetation Maps,* edited by A.W. Kuchler (OCLC #294799), covering all of North and South America, Africa, Asia, Australia, and the U.S.S.R., is available for use. Most maps are accompanied by full descriptive texts.

McGuffey Collection of School Textbooks. An excellent resource for American social history and the history of education, the collection is composed of manuscript materials relating to William Holmes McGuffey, the most complete set of McGuffey Readers in the country, and some 5,000 19th-century American school textbooks covering all subject areas.

George Orwell Collection. In addition to his other works, the collection includes the first appearance in print of many Orwell essays and articles in such periodicals as *The Adelphi* and *The Partisan Review.*

Paper Science Collection. Over 2,000 bound journals and 3,000 books cover the history and theory of papermaking as well as current research.

Samuel Richey Collection of the Southern Confederacy. A comprehensive collection of both original manuscripts and secretarial copies covering the correspondence of Confederate President Jefferson Davis, his wife, his generals, and cabinet members.

Andre L. de Saint-Rat Collection. This collection, containing approximately 2,000 volumes on Russian history, literature, and art, focuses on 19th-century Russian military history. It includes scarce regimental histories, volumes from the Romanov personal libraries, and some extremely rare works not otherwise available outside the Soviet Union.

Shaker Collection. This group of approximately 250 items includes books, music, and ephemera relating to the history and study of Shakerism.

World Culinary Collection. Over 3,000 bound volumes from the 18th century to the present, with emphasis on American regional cooking.

Oberlin College Library (OBE)
Oberlin, OH

Edwin Arlington Robinson Collection. The collection includes almost all of Robinson's first appearances in print in many variant editions, both poems and prose. Also included are books about Robinson, biographies, criticisms, and interpretations. There are manuscript letters and miscellaneous materials, such as photographs of Robinson's house and clippings of reviews from newspapers. 156 titles representing 189 volumes have been cataloged.

OCLC Library (OCC)
Dublin, OH

Data Processing Manuals Collection. Approximately 3,000 titles in this hardware and software manual collection are housed and circulated from the OCLC Documentation Library, which has been profiled as a separate holding library (OCCD). The primary vendor series within the collection and approximate number of titles are: IBM (1,400), Tandem Computers (290), Data General (158), Xerox/Honeywell (140), Apollo (80), SAS (70), SUN (70), Tolerant (60), Digital Equipment Corp. (55), and Convergent Technologies (35).

Library Network Newsletter Collection. The extensive collection of library network newsletters includes publications from networks providing OCLC services (e.g., AMIGOS and SUNY), as well as from the Research Libraries Group (RLG), Western Library Network (WLN), and Cooperative Library Agency for Systems and Services (CLASS). As of April 1987, this collection included 170 titles.

State Library and State Library Association Newsletters. This newest special collection, begun in 1986, contains newsletters from state library agencies and associations. The ordering and processing of this collection is still underway, but the collection currently contains 30 state library newsletters and 18 state library association newsletters. Publications from all states are on order.

Ohioana Library (MCU)
Columbus, OH

A 30,000 book collection of works by Ohioans or about Ohio, many in first editions, includes one of the most complete collections of the works of William Dean Howells in existence. Many works are self-published memoirs or poetry, and there are a number of Ph.D. dissertations as well.

Ohio Historical Society Archives (OHT)
Columbus, OH

A collection of 3,000 Ohio newspapers includes 13 issues of one of Ohio's earliest newspapers, the *Ohio Star and New-Richmond and Suzanna Gazette,* believed to be the only surviving issues of the paper, published over 160 years ago. The society also has a large George Armstrong Custer collection and an Ohio photo collection.

The Ohio State University (OSU)
Columbus, OH

William Charvat American Fiction Collection. The collection contains 10,000 American fiction titles published between 1901 and 1925. More than 6,000 of these titles are already cataloged on the OCLC database. All books receive full rare book cataloging according to the rules of the Library of Congress as found in its manual, *Bibliographic Description of Rare Books.* Access points are provided for illustrators, binding designers, publishers, and printers, making the collection more readily available not only to literary scholars but to art historians and scholars interested in printing history. A discrete machine-readable tape of this portion of the cataloging for the Charvat Collection will be available nationally at the conclusion of the project.

Hilandar Research Library. Microfilmed manuscripts, principally assembled from the Hilandar Monastery library on Mt. Athos, Greece, represent a 1,000-item repository of Slavic literature and culture. Over 90% of the total Slavic literature produced from the 9th century to date has been destroyed by time or natural or manmade events, so these microfilms not only make the information more available but serve to protect it from eventual decay. Much of the collection is liturgical, and there are color prints of original illustrations. Over 2,000 manuscripts from 16 countries in 14 languages are represented.

Historical Children's Literature and Curriculum Collection. This collection consists of 350 volumes representing children's literature and curriculum materials of historic interest. In addition to older materials, the collection recently added a portion of the Garland facsimiles of children's literature and has also acquired the recently published Osborne Collection facsimiles.

Rare Books and Manuscripts and the James Thurber Reading Room. In addition to the works of Columbus native Thurber, this collection includes 80 busts of famous authors (Carl Sandburg, Amelia Earhart, and James Joyce among them) donated by Gale Research Company. There are also 350 letters from Simone de Beauvoir to her lover, Chicago novelist Nelson Algren, and papers of Ohio poet Hart Crane.

Ohio University Libraries (OUN)
Athens, OH

Author Collections. Thirty-three authors, English for the most part, are represented by this collection. Periods represented are 1750–1850 and 1880–1930. The collections exemplify the transition from classicism to romanticism in English poetry and the rise of realism in the English novel. The following authors are represented by first and other early editions: Thomas Campbell (17 titles), William Cowper (68), George Crabbe (17), Thomas Hood (54), Leigh Hunt (58), and Samuel Rogers (78). The collections of works by Tennyson (372 titles) and Ruskin (94) are particularly impressive. Among late 19th- and early 20th-century authors are works by W.H. Davies (73 titles), Wilfred Gibson (44), W.W. Jacobs (17), Ronald Firbank (27), Arthur Machen (33), William Watson (59), H.G. Wells (277), and Rudyard Kipling (166).

Local Government Records Collection. Ohio University is one of several repositories in the Ohio Network of American History Research Centers. The library houses well over 1,000 linear feet of records created by agencies of county, city, and township government in an 18-county region of southeastern Ohio, from the early 1800s to date. A printed *Guide to Local Government Records in the Ohio University Library* (OCLC #8863816) is available.

Manuscript Collections. Collections comprising some 1,215 linear feet, developed with a view toward collecting the papers of individuals, families, businesses, and organizations important to the history of southeastern Ohio. Includes botanical notebooks of Manasseh Cutler; personal papers of many settlers and their families; records of churches, fraternal organizations, literary societies and debating clubs, workingmen's associations and labor unions (particularly the United Mine Workers of America); as well as more than 20 other smaller collections from unions in southeastern Ohio. Other areas of collecting include papers of Ohio artists, writers, and musicians and records of the Ohio Osteopathic Association.

The J.W. Morgan Collection in the History of Chemistry. Some 1,400 books by famous 16th–20th century chemists, mostly in first editions. Figures represented in depth include Robert Boyle, Joseph Priestley, Michael Faraday, William Harvey, William Henry, Antoine Lavoisier, Justus Liebig, and James Watt. Certain subject areas related to chemistry, such as medicine and alchemy, are also represented. Although the Morgan Collection is largely uncataloged, a printed short-title catalog (OCLC #266015) is available.

Ohioana Collection. Well over 1,000 printed books, mostly old and rare, on the history of Ohio, the Upper Ohio River Valley, and the Trans-Allegheny migration. Includes early accounts of travel, maps, memoirs of settlers, early imprints and literature, and works on nearly every aspect of the region's natural, political, cultural, and social history.

Osteopathic Medicine Collection. Relatively comprehensive collection of the literature of osteopathic medicine published prior to 1940.

Cornelius Ryan Collection of World War II Papers. This collection (OCLC #9635542) contains original manuscripts, correspondence, photographs, and other material documenting the history of World War II, with an emphasis on the personal papers of working journalists. Included are the manuscripts, correspondence, and extensive research files for each of Ryan's major books on World War II: *The Longest Day* (1959), *The Last Battle* (1966), and *A Bridge Too Far* (1974). Some 21,000 research files are present, of which at least 7,000 contain transcribed interviews and correspondence with individual participants. The files are organized into three groups, corresponding to the three books, further subdivided according to the nationality of those being interviewed. All interviews have been translated into English and are often supplemented by diaries, diary extracts, and field reports transcribed from official documents. In addition, the collection contains extensive photographic files, nearly 100 maps, and copies of Ryan's original manuscripts in various stages of revision. A detailed inventory of the collection is available for the use of researchers.

Southeast Asia Collection. Approximately 90,000 titles covering the countries of Southeast Asia: Brunei, Burma, Cambodia, Indonesia, Malaysia, Philippines, Singapore, Thailand, and Vietnam. Includes vernacular languages of insular Southeast Asia. The collection is a repository for Malaysian documents. Most of the titles have been cataloged in the OCLC database and are available for interlibrary loan.

University of Cincinnati (CIN)
Cincinnati, OH

Burnam Classical Library. One of the largest collections in the world of materials relating to all aspects of Greek and Roman antiquity, this collection consists of over 80,000 volumes. There is an additional microfilm collection of 13,500 pamphlets, dissertations, and *Programmschriften* from the 18th and 19th centuries and a collection of some 5,000 volumes relating to Greek and Latin paleography. One half of this library's Modern Greek Collection, consisting of an additional 25,000 volumes, has also been converted onto OCLC in order to include titles of interest to Classicists and Byzantinists, including music, art, religion and philosophy, bibliography, anthropology, and geology.

Elliston Poetry Collection. The collection was established in 1951 as a collection of 20th century, English-language poetry from the United States, Great Britain, Canada, and Australia. Today it numbers approximately 10,000 volumes of poetry, including small collections of rare books, broadsides, records, and a growing cassette tape archive of over 350 original poetry readings; its periodical subscriptions number 150.

University of Cincinnati Medical Center (MXC)
Cincinnati, OH

These collections are housed at Historical, Archival, and Museum Services:

Dennis E. Jackson Pharmacology Collection. A collection of 500 titles on pharmacology and related subjects. Collected and donated by Dr. Jackson, who invented a machine to facilitate anesthesia with carbon dioxide absorption in 1914.

The Cecil Striker Collection. A collection of 900 titles with emphasis on diabetes and the history of medicine.

David A. Tucker, Jr. Library of the History of Medicine. Over 1,600 volumes supporting the study of the history of medicine range in subject matter from 16th-century herbals to modern biographies.

These collections are housed at the Nursing Educational Resources Library:

Phoebe M. Kandel History of Nursing Collection. Over 2,000 volumes of early 20th-century nursing and public health materials.

Boston Collection. So-named because the Boston Medical Library Classification system is used, the collection consists of approximately 7,000 volumes with imprint dates from 1921–1965. It includes classic works in all areas of clinical medicine and related branches of science.

Urbana College (URB)
Urbana, OH

Swedenborg Collection. Holdings, consisting of approximately 2,000 titles, include books in various languages by and about Emanuel Swedenborg, John Chapman (Johnny Appleseed), Helen Keller, and other Swedenborgians. The collection also includes periodicals and other publications of the General Convention of the New Jerusalem in the United States of America (the New Jerusalem Church) and its affiliates. Urbana College Library is retrospectively converting this collection in honor of Emanuel Swedenborg's upcoming 300th birthday anniversary.

Unused cover idea for My Life and Hard Times, *from the James Thurber Collection, Division of Special Collections, The Ohio State University Libraries.*

Wright State University (WSU)
Dayton, OH

The Wright Brothers Collection. This aviation collection consists of manuscripts, photographs, monographs, and serials, which originally were part of the Wright brothers' personal library. There are 42 monographic titles and 17 serial titles comprising the 84 volumes in this collection. Works are in English, German, and French.

Wright State University Health Sciences Library (WSH)
Dayton, OH

Greene County Medical Society Collection. A collection of 43 microfiche, consisting of the minutes (1888–1958), *The Bulletin of the Greene County Medical Society,* and miscellaneous records.

The Ross A. McFarland Collection in Aerospace Medicine and Human Factors Engineering. More than 6,000 books, journals, and technical reports that comprise the print portion of the collection have been cataloged. Manuscripts have also been input.

The Thelma Fordham Pruett Rare Book Room Collection. Consists chiefly of 18th and 19th century American imprints. There are presently 225 titles.

Linfield College (OLC)
McMinnville, OR

The Baptist Collection. In addition to 35 volumes of monographs, the collection includes approximately 750 volumes of serials, among them various 19th and early 20th century Baptist periodicals, as well as minutes and reports of annual meetings of various local and regional Baptist associations and organizations. The manuscript collection also includes some 50 volumes of official records, dating back to 1844, of churches and church organizations in the Portland (Oregon) area.

Southwestern Oregon Community College (SWO)
Coos Bay, OR

The Swearingen Collection. Originally owned by a music critic for the *St. Louis Post Dispatch,* this collection of 650 classical records was donated by Dr. Jack Swearingen of Brownsville, OR. Consisting primarily of 78-rpm recordings produced in the 1930s and 1940s, the collection includes performances by most of the well-known artists of the era, some of whom have autographed their works. Also included are a few 33⅓-rpm recordings circa 1949–1951. The disks have been reproduced on cassettes for circulation.

Alliance College (PCS)
Cambridge Springs, PA

The Polish Collection. One of the largest devoted to Polish Studies in the United States. Numbering approximately 20,000 pieces, it includes some 2,000 pamphlets of limited distribution published by many small Polish American associations, clubs, groups, and parishes.

The Athenaeum (PAT)
Philadelphia, PA

The Reeve Fox Hunting Collection. Includes nonfiction and fiction on fox hunting in England and America, the latter focusing on the Philadelphia area. Approximately 200 monographic titles have been cataloged on OCLC.

The Rupp Transportation Collection. Approximately 1,000 monographic items, 700 of which are cataloged on OCLC. It focuses on the history of American transportation, chiefly railroads, and includes 19th and 20th century items.

Bucknell University (PBU)
Lewisburg, PA

D.H. Lawrence Collection. Lawrence's first editions, consisting of about 120 items.

Cabrini College (PAB)
Radnor, PA

Franklin Delano Roosevelt Collection. Books and journals (243 titles) by or about FDR and his administration.

Duquesne University (DUQ)
Pittsburgh, PA

Herman Hailperin Collection. Emphasizes materials on Judeo-Christian relations during the Middle Ages.

The Simon Silverman Phenomenology Center Collection. The world's most complete collection of literature, published and unpublished, on the subject of phenomenology (a contemporary movement in philosophy, psychology, and other human sciences). The collection includes as "alcoves" the personal libraries of prominent phenomenologists. Nearly half of the 5,200 volumes have been entered into OCLC.

The Free Library of Philadelphia (PLF)
Philadelphia, PA

The Rare Book Department of the Free Library of Philadelphia is one of the largest among pubic libraries in the U.S. Its holdings span a period of more than 4,000 years, from Sumerian cuneiform tables (the world's oldest "books") to modern fine printing. The library's first gift of rare books was received in 1899, when the institution was only five years old. Others followed through the years and in 1949 the bequest of the entire private library of William McIntire Elkins, together with the paneled room that housed it, led to the opening of the Rare Book Department. Among the collections are:

Charles Dickens Collection. The Dickens holdings include a wealth of association items: the author's desk and its appointments, over 1,000 of the novelist's letters, and the original manuscript of *The Life of Our Lord,* the manuscript Dickens felt was of such personal significance that it was never published in his lifetime or his children's.

European Manuscripts. This collection of manuscripts from the 9th–18th centuries is further supported by a group of books dealing with European and American calligraphy, together with many original calligraphic specimens. **Oriental Manuscripts** and more than 1,200 Oriental miniatures, largely Mughul, Persian, and Rajput, are included. There is considerable emphasis on early printing and a wide representation of the 15th-century presses of continental Europe.

The Growth and Development of Common Law. A comprehensive collection assembled by noted Philadelphia lawyer Hampton L. Carson begins with manuscripts of Magna Carta about the year 1300 and continues to the present. The 16th-century holdings and editions of Blackstone are outstanding. The collection also contains thousands of legal prints and documents and letters of lawyers and jurists.

Edgar Allan Poe Collection. Rich in manuscripts and autograph letters, this collection includes copies of all the first editions of Poe's works. The rarest of the printed pieces are the *Tamerlane* of 1827, one of 11 copies known, and the *Balloon Hoax* of 1844, one of two copies known.

Pennsylvania German Collections include more than 1,000 of the colorful manuscripts known as fraktur.

Early American Children's Books. Fragile volumes date from 1682–1836 and include the historical collection of the *American Sunday-School Union,* presented by the Union itself. The present century is represented by the **Robert Lawson** collection, which includes more than 1,100 originals of illustrations by Lawson, many of his papers, and his own copies of books he illustrated. Among the drawings are the earliest for *The Story of Ferdinand* by Munro Leaf, to which Mrs. Leaf has added the original manuscript.

There are three outstanding collections of English origin. The **Beatrix Potter Collection** contains over 100 of her original drawings and water colors, the original manuscripts of *The Tailor of Gloucester* and *Little Pig Robinson,* and all of her first editions.

The Arthur Rackham Collection includes original water colors and drawings, limited and trade editions, and periodical appearances of Rackham's illustrations.

The Kate Greenaway Collection of original water colors, first editions, letters, and ephemerae.

The Howard Pyle Collection is also rich in original paintings, drawings, and first editions.

Another delightful collection of an illustrator is that of **A.B. Frost.**

Gettysburg College (GDC)
Gettysburg, PA

Civil War Collection. This 2,500-title collection focuses primarily on the Battle of Gettysburg, but the collection also includes regimental histories, personal reminiscences, diaries, government publications, and local histories.

The H.L. Mencken Collection. This collection of 625 titles consists primarily of first editions and first appearances (in periodicals, etc.) of Mencken. The collection also includes material by Fitzgerald, Hemingway, Dreiser, and Hammett.

The Haverford School (HVF)
Haverford, PA

The George Rehrauer Film Study Collection. 5,791 books from the personal collection of Rehrauer, a noted film bibliographer. The collection contains hundreds of general histories of the movies; biographies of actors, directors and producers; anthologies; bibliographies; interviews; criticism; business aspects of the film industry; filmmaking (production, direction, script writing, cinematography, etc.); genre studies; general reference (i.e., almanacs); screenplays; sociology of film (effect of film viewing, censorship, etc.); and study guides.

Lehigh University (LYU)
Bethlehem, PA

The Special Collections division consists of more than 20,000 volumes comprising a wide variety of material, including about a dozen incunabula. Areas of strength include the history of science and technology and 18th- and 19th-century English and American literature. Among specific areas of strength are ornithology (including the Audubon elephant folio *Birds of America*) and Charles Darwin. The collection is also strong in the works of Mark Twain and James Fenimore Cooper.

Lincoln University (LZU)
Lincoln University, PA

African and Afro-American Collection. 760 titles, many of which were published during the 18th and 19th centuries. Subject strengths include Afro-Americans, Africans, religion, slavery, history, and literature. Many titles are associated with a special person or event of importance. Examples include a first edition of *Poems* by Phillis Wheatley (1773) and a presentation copy of *Ghana* by Kwame Nkrumah, class of 1939.

Millersville University of Pennsylvania (MVS)
Millersville, PA

Leo Ascher Center for the Study of Operetta Music. The Ascher collection houses materials by Ascher and eight of his contemporaries: Paul Abraham, Edmund Eysler, Leo Fall, Bruno Grandichstaedten, Emmerich Kalman, Franz Lehar, Robert Stolz, and Oscar Straus.

Colonial Research Collection. Includes reprints of the archives of the colonies and related materials that have significance as primary research materials.

Living Pennsylvania Composers Collection. A depository for living composers' compositions that are performable by school musicians. Contains scores and tapes of unpublished compositions only.

Pennsylvania Research Collection. Materials in a variety of forms written by Pennsylvanians or about the Commonwealth, with emphasis on Lancaster and surrounding counties. Includes a microfilm edition of all 19th-century histories and atlases of the counties and materials on the history and culture of the Pennsylvania Germans and other pioneers in the area.

Wickersham Pedagogical Collection. Pre-1900 textbooks, books on methods, and periodicals dealing with the art of teaching.

Philadelphia College of Textiles & Science (PCT)
Philadelphia, PA

Textile Industry Historical Collection. This special collection encompasses all aspects of the American textile industry during the 19th and early 20th centuries. The object is the development of a research collection including all materials printed in English relevant to the textile industry. Over 2,500 volumes, many of which have been entered on OCLC. Also includes over 50 textile journals published prior to 1940.

Of special interest is material focusing on the development of the Philadelphia textile industry. To supplement this secondary material, original business records of local textile firms are actively sought. The historical collection includes business records, correspondence, and diaries related to over 10 different Philadelphia textile companies. Also sought are photographs of textile companies, personal diaries of textile workers, and advertising ephemera related to the textile industry in the Philadelphia area.

Pittsburgh Theological Seminary (PKT)
Pittsburgh, PA

The Anderson Rare Book Collection. 4,203 titles (6,273 volumes) containing classical theological works dating from the Reformation.

The Warrington Hymnology Collection. Over 1,800 hymn and song books from the estate of James Warrington of Philadelphia provide research materials for scholars of American and English hymnody.

Rosemont College (RMC)
Rosemont, PA

Early Pennsylvania History Collection. This collection of 726 volumes of pre-1860 Pennsylvania history, built around the complete set of 138 volumes of Colonial records and the Pennsylvania archives, includes materials by persons living in this time period as well as by later writers on pre-Civil War Pennsylvania.

Published according to Act of Parliament, Sept. 1, 1773 by Arch.ᵈ ℐ
Bookseller Nᵒ 8 near the Saracens Head Aldgate.

P O E M S

O N

VARIOUS SUBJECTS,

RELIGIOUS AND MORAL.

ʙ ʏ

PHILLIS WHEATLEY,

NEGRO SERVANT to Mr. JOHN WHEATLEY,
of BOSTON, in NEW ENGLAND.

L O N D O N:
Printed for A. Bᴇʟʟ, Bookseller, Aldgate; and sold by
Messrs. Cox and Bᴇʀʀʏ, King-Street, BOSTON.
M DCC LXXIII.

Title page and frontispiece from the University of Rochester copy of Phillis Wheat-
ley's Poems on Various Subjects, Religious and Moral, *published in London in 1773.*

U.S. Army Military History Institute (MHR)
Carlisle Barracks, PA

Army Unit History Collection. About 3,000 titles, comprising histories of the United States Army (Regular Army) units since 1900.

University of Pennsylvania (SPG)
Philadelphia, PA

Spanish Drama of the Golden Age. A microform collection of 4,393 plays and other literary genres, including loas, autos sacramentales, and poems by major dramatists of the Golden Age (1500–1700) and modern compilations published in the 19th century.

University of Pittsburgh (PIT)
Pittsburgh, PA

The Bolivian Pamphlet Collection. Over 1,000 pamphlets, 6,800 monographs, and 110 serial titles constitute this valuable and unique collection covering a wide variety of topics from the 19th and 20th centuries. The major focus is on politics and government, but economics, history, agriculture, education, and sociology, among others, are covered as well. For purposes of preservation, the collection will be transferred to microfilm. Microfiche copies of items will be accessible through interlibrary loan or by purchase.

John A. Nietz Textbook Collection. Consists of approximately 15,000 volumes and is one of the three largest collections of pre-1900 American textbooks in the U.S. Within this collection are textbooks on every imaginable school subject—from algebra and arithmetic to storybooks and zoology—ranging from the 18th to the early 20th century. A Title II-C project to catalog the Nietz Collection on OCLC was completed in the fall of 1987.

Rhode Island Historical Society Library (RDS)
Providence, RI

Film Archives. A quarter million feet of film and videotape in a variety of formats: PSAs, home movies, features, and TV newsfilm. Most of the film is 16mm newsfilm, but the archives include some early 28.5mm footage. The archives reflect both the history of Rhode Island and the state's role in the evolution of motion pictures in the U.S. The collection presently includes events recorded by Thomas Edison in the early 1900s, professional feature films made in Rhode Island in the 1920s, national newsreels in the 1930s and 1940s, local television newsfilm and documentaries from the 1950s to date, and equipment, scrapbooks, publicity stills, and theater business records. To gain control over this material and provide better access, in 1983 the Society started a recataloging project using the OCLC audiovisual format.

Clemson University (SEA)
Clemson, SC

Betsy (Cromer) Byars Collection. Foreign-language translations and English-language editions of children's literature by this Carolina author are cataloged in OCLC.

Francis Marion College (SFM)
Florence, SC

The George Alfred Henty Collection. This collection of 141 volumes includes 95 of the titles written by George Alfred Henty (1832–1902), popular English author of adventure stories for boys. In many instances the library holds both the original English and the first American editions. The collection also includes works about Henty.

The Small Arms Technical Publishing Company Collection. This collection of 48 volumes includes most of the titles on hunting and firearms published by Thomas Samworth (1888–1981), onetime editor of *The American Rifleman,* who spent the better part of his career living on a rice plantation in nearby Plantersville.

South Carolina State College (ISO)
Orangeburg, SC

Black Culture and History Collection. The Miller F. Whittaker Library's special collection of black culture and history contains 12,000 titles. It was formerly called "The Negro Alumni Collection."

Augustana College (SDA)
Sioux Falls, SD

Herbert Krause Collection. This 12,000-volume collection includes a wide assortment of English and American literary works, many of which are first editions. Works on American history, with an emphasis on the history of the western region and native Americans, comprise another facet. The third portion deals with ornithology. An avid birdwatcher and traveler, Dr. Krause collected books relating to ornithology around the world.

The Krause Collection is part of a library of 30,000 volumes dealing primarily with Northern Plains and Western American history and culture that includes such publications as the *South Dakota History Collections, Collections of the State Historical Society of North Dakota, Minnesota Historical Collections, Nebraska State Historical Society Collections, Jesuit Relations and Allied Documents,* and *Original Journals of the Lewis and Clark Expedition.* There are also 1,500 cubic feet of archives and manuscripts collections, including the archives of the Episcopal Diocese of South Dakota, the American Lutheran Church South Dakota District, the United Church of Christ South Dakota Conference, personal papers of business, professional, and literary people, and county and state records.

Dakota Wesleyan University (SDW)
Mitchell, SD

Jennewein Western Library Collection. Approximately 4,800 volumes, containing South Dakota and Middle Border history and literature, including American Indian legends, literature, and history.

Sioux Falls College (SDF)
Sioux Falls, SD

South Dakota Collection. Approximately 1,000 books, about 250 in reference, about South Dakota, as well as works by South Dakota authors.

University of South Dakota (USD)
Vermillion, SD

Herman P. Chilson Western American Collection. The 20,000 units in this collection are a major resource for South Dakota material, containing significant holdings on Native Americans, specifically the Sioux, as well as resources for other areas of the northern Great Plains, e.g., North Dakota, Minnesota, particularly west central Minnesota, Wyoming, Montana, and Nebraska.

Chattanooga-Hamilton County Bicentennial Library (TCH)
Chattanooga, TN

Historical Collection. 11,019 volumes. A collection of compiled genealogies including the southeastern states, with emphasis on the eastern counties of Tennessee. The collection also includes county records and county histories, federal census records 1790 –1880, and material dealing with Hamilton County (the county in which Chattanooga is located). Considerable material on New England, Pennsylvania, and Maryland genealogy and history is also included.

Tennessee Room. 13,478 volumes. A collection with general emphasis on Tennessee history and special attention to materials pertaining to the life, history, and culture of the city of Chattanooga.

East Tennessee State University (MET)
Quillen-Dishner College of Medicine Library
Johnson City, TN

The Long Collection. Contains approximately 2,000 medical volumes from the late 19th and early 20th centuries. Donated by local surgeon Dr. Carroll Long, the books were collected by his father Dr. E. A. Long, also of Johnson City, and his uncle, Dr. John Andrew Hardy of El Paso, TX.

Lee College (TLC)
Cleveland, TN

Church of God and Church Pentecostal Collections. There are 1,989 titles in the Church of God collection and 2,991 titles in the Church Pentecostal Collection. It is the goal and purpose of the library to maintain an extensive collection of information at a research level about the Church of God and about Pentecostalism. Materials available include monographs, periodicals, nonbook materials, and information files.

Nashville Public Library (TNN)
Nashville, TN

Hearing Impaired Collection. Books for people with hearing problems and for people with a special interest in hearing problems. 800 volumes.

Large-print Collections. Books printed in large type, centered in the main library and the four largest branches, with a rotating collection set up as a ''holding library'' with its own OCLC symbol. 1,250 titles.

Nashville Authors Collection. Books by authors who are, or have been, Nashvillians. 1,300 volumes.

Tennesseana. Tennessee history, with emphasis on the Nashville area in middle Tennessee. 7,000 volumes.

Weil Ornithological Collection. Books, journals, daily diaries of bird sightings, and personal notes assembled over a period of 60 years by Henry C. Monk, of Nashville. Ongoing book collection entered in database. 300 volumes.

Tennessee Valley Authority (TVA)
Knoxville, TN

Forestry and Natural Resources Collection. 8,000 volumes of materials related to forestry, fisheries and aquatic ecology, wildlife development, environmental education, and recreation.

National Fertilizer and Development Collection. One of the most complete collections (6,200 volumes) on the history, production, and use of fertilizers. Subject em-

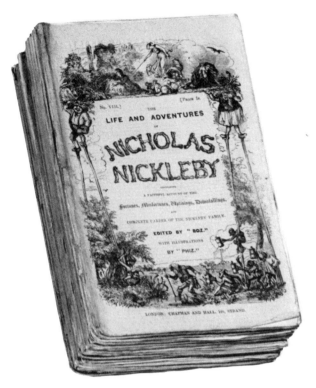

Nichalos Nickleby *in parts (1838–39), by Charles Dickens, from the Ulizio Collection, Kent State University.*

Incas (including the King and Queen of Peru) and vase forms found in tombs. From A Voyage to the South-Sea, and Along the Coasts of Chili and Peru, in the Years 1712, 1713, and 1714. . . , *Wm. Charters South Seas Collection, Butler University.*

phasis on agriculture, chemistry, chemical engineering, economics, and impact of fertilizer technology on developing countries.

Tennessee Valley Authority Collection. 15,000 volumes of materials relating to the history and development of the TVA and the Tennessee River Valley. This includes TVA publications and materials needed to support TVA programs. Subject emphasis includes flood control and navigation, power production and public utilities, engineering (civil, mechanical, electrical, and nuclear), regional planning and resource development, and energy research and development.

Tusculum College (TCL)
Greeneville, TN

Charles Coffin Collection. Approximately 2,000 volumes dating from the 16th century through 1829. The collection represents the surviving library of the oldest chartered college west of the Alleghenies (Greeneville College, which was succeeded by Tusculum College) as well as the only surviving library from a postrevolutionary frontier college.

The University of Tennessee (TKN)
Knoxville, TN

Early Imprints. In addition to examples from Tennessee's early presses, the collection proudly claims a 1481 edition of Cicero's *De Officiis* and another incunabulum, *Biblia Integra,* printed in 1495. The incunabula (works printed before 1501) are accompanied by an array of 16th and 17th-century imprints from the presses of continental Europe and Great Britain.

The Early Voyages and Travels Collection. This collection includes the 1814 edition of *History of the Expedition Under the Command of Captains Lewis and Clark,* a facsimile of *The Log of H.M.S. Bounty,* the 1712 edition of Captain Cooke's *A Voyage to the South Sea, Travels to the Westward of the Allegany Mountains* (1805) by Andre Michaux, John Bradbury's *Travels in the Interior of America* (1819), and *Early Travels in the Tennessee Country* by Samuel Cole Williams.

The 19th Century American Literature Collections. First editions include works of Harriet Beecher Stowe, Nathaniel Hawthorne, James Fenimore Cooper, Walt Whitman, Ernest Hemingway, Washington Irving, Mark Twain, Henry James, and Herman Melville.

North American Indian Collection. This collection includes a file of *The Cherokee Phoenix,* an Indian newspaper printed in both Cherokee characters and English; a complete run of the *Cherokee Almanac;* first editions of James Adair's *History of the American Indians* and *Memoirs of Lieut. Henry Timberlake*; compilations of early laws of the Cherokees; books of the Bible, songsters, and other works printed in the Cherokee language; and original color prints of a number of Cherokee chieftains.

The Rare Book Collection. Some 25,000 volumes include books dating from 1481 to the present. There are also definitive collections of the works of William Congreve and Jane Austen.

Tennessee Collection. Items include the Roulstone imprints, rare and unique examples from the press of Tennessee's first printer George Roulstone, first printings of the historical treatises of John Haywood and J.G.M. Ramsey, the earliest issues of the Davy Crockett Almanacs, early maps of the Southwest Territory and Tennessee, the first compilations of the Acts and Journals of the Tennessee legislature; and original editions of works produced by the state's leading literary figures.

Vanderbilt University Library (TJC)
Nashville, TN

Baudelaire Center Collection. 6,000 titles of works by and relating to French poet and critic Charles Baudelaire (1821–1867), translator of Edgar Allen Poe. Complemented by an exhaustive gathering of ephemeral material, this collection allows researchers to pursue economically and thoroughly studies in Baudelaire, Poe, comparative literature, French studies, art criticism, music, and psychology.

Pascal Pia Collection. This collection of 20,000 volumes comprises the library of the eminent French man of letters, who was an associate of Gide and Nerval, advisor to Malraux, and sponsor of Camus. The collection provides extensive coverage of 20th century French literature and art, with additional special emphasis on censored material, surrealism, the occult, erotica, and curiosa.

Wills Fugitive/Agrarian Collection. 1,000 titles of works by the poets and about the Nashville-based literary movement of the 1920s, the major figures of which were associated with the "New Criticism." Donald Davidson, John Crowe Ransom, Allen Tate, and Robert Penn Warren also focused resistance to the industrialization of the South, publishing with others in 1930 the Agrarian Manifesto, *I'll Take My Stand.* The special collections also hold papers relating to individual members and the two groups.

Houston Academy of Medicine, Texas Medical Center Library (TMC)
Houston, TX

John P. McGovern History of Medicine Collection. Nearly 2,000 titles concentrate on the development of American medicine and the medical specialities from 1840–1920. There is emphasis on collecting American publishers, particularly William Wood & Co. The collection also contains nearly 300 titles on French medicine from 1730–1830 and over 100 titles on cardiovascular diseases and surgery. Seminal works from British publishers, along with the translations and classics from the Sydenham and New Sydenham Societies, complement the American and French portions of the collection.

Lamar University (TXR)
Beaumont, TX

The Justice Cookery Collection. Assembled by Philip S. Justice, an executive with Sun Oil, this collection totals 563 volumes dating from around 1500 to 1900. The collection is particularly strong in English and American cookbooks of the 19th century. The rarest item in the collection is Coelius Apicius' *De re Coquinaria* published in Venice circa 1499.

Southern Methodist University, Central Library (ISM)
Dallas, TX

The Stewart Irvin Oost Collection. The Oost Collection, consisting of over 5,000 volumes, has been called "the largest private classics collection in the United States" and includes monographs, dissertations, pamphlets, reprints, reference and collected works, government publications, and some periodical runs. The earliest imprint identified is 1541. The materials are printed in at least fifteen languages.

Southern Methodist University, DeGolyer Library (FKS)
Dallas, TX

Fondren-Clampitt Collection of Texana. The collection (1,125 titles) covers the whole range of Texas subjects but emphasizes general, county, and literary histories; biographies; and cookbooks, as well as books by Texas authors and works on wildflowers, birds, and hunting.

Southwestern University (TXX)
Georgetown, TX

Edward E. Clark Australia Collection. Collected during the time that Mr. Clark was ambassador to Australia in the 1960s, this collection of 240 titles is a good source of basic printed materials. It includes works on natural history, social life and customs, art, literature, ethnology, and history.

Edward E. Clark Burr Collection. A collection of 49 printed works on Aaron Burr's life, career, trials, and memoirs.

Edward E. Clark Texana Collection. 7,092 titles based on a private collection rich in basic printed source material for the period of the Republic (1836–1845), the annexation (1845), and the reconstruction (1865) period. There is also a large collection of printed, manuscript, and photographic material of Georgetown and Williamson County.

The Isabel Gaddis Collection. This collection of 542 titles is rich in early James Frank Dobie material, including contributions made to the university's yearbook, *Sou'wester,* proof copies and manuscripts of many of his books, and a complete collection of all of his printed works. In addition, the collection contains manuscripts with changes and corrections in Dobie's handwriting, as well as holographs and notes to his editors.

Jackson-Greenwood Collection. Consists of 5,381 English and American 19th century literary titles.

Texana Collection. This 1,700-title collection contains basic source material on Texas, Southwestern University, Williamson County, and Georgetown, Texas. Both printed and photographic material are included in the collection.

Texas A & M University (TXA)
College Station, TX

Jeff Dykes Range Livestock Collection. About 60% of this collection of approximately 18,000 titles has been entered in OCLC. The works are principally in English, Spanish, and French and cover virtually every facet of the range livestock industry worldwide.

Great Western Illustrators Collection. The approximately 5,000 titles in this collection represent the published works of over 50 illustrators of the American West.

Ku Klux Klan Collection. This historical collection includes ephemera as well as over 300 monographs and serials illustrating the Reconstruction Klan and the Klan of the 1920s.

Science Fiction Research Collection. About 40% of this collection of over 18,000 serial and monograph titles and manuscripts on science fiction and fantasy has been entered in OCLC.

Texas College of Osteopathic Medicine (TOM)
Fort Worth, TX

The Osteopathic Historical Book Collection. This collection of nearly 1,000 volumes documents the founding, growth, and development of osteopathic medicine. To meet this goal, all materials related to osteopathic medicine and/or those written by osteopathic physicians are being collected as comprehensively as possible. Related subject areas, such as orthopedic manipulation, massage, bonesetting, and chiropractic, are also emphasized. To place osteopathic medicine in historical perspective, representative medical works are being collected to illustrate the state of medical knowledge and education in late 19th and early 20th century America. Secondary works in the history of American medicine provide support for the collection. Landmark works in the history of medicine are provided through reprints.

Texas Southern University (TXT)
Houston, TX

The Heartman Collection on Negro Life and Culture. The nucleus of the collection was purchased in 1948 from a German-born bookdealer, Charles F. Heartman of Biloxi, Mississippi. The collection contains books, pamphlets, lithographs, oil paintings, musical scores, almanacs, diaries, Texas slave narratives, scrapbooks, and other documents specifically pertaining to the growth and development of Black people in Texas, the United States, and the world. It is considered the largest and most comprehensive research collection on Blacks to be found in the southwest United States. Nearly a quarter of the 25,000-title collection has been entered in OCLC.

Texas Tech University (ILU)
Lubbock, TX

The Joseph Conrad Collection. This 373-title collection includes British and American first editions of each of Conrad's works. It is one of the most complete collections of the printed states of Conrad's works available in the world.

The Dalhousie Manuscripts. These manuscripts containing poems by John Donne and some of his contemporaries are thought to be ones for which the copyist had access to Donne's own—no longer extant—copies of the poems and, hence, are of critical importance in establishing an authoritative text.

The Samuel Wieselberg Autographs Collection. Approximately 400 items including books, manuscripts, and photographs. The manuscripts include a letter from Queen Isabella of Spain to her daughter, a Continental Army release signed by General Washington, and several documents signed by Napoleon and his marshals.

The University of Texas at Austin (IXA)
Austin, TX

Aldine Collection. Five hundred editions from the press of Aldo Manuzio and his successors, Venice, 1495–1592.

Benson Latin American Collection Serials List. This first microfiche edition of the *Benson Latin American Collection Serials List* and its *Indexes* incorporates the 23,600 serial titles and their 77,000 bound holdings shelved in the Collection that have matching OCLC bibliographic records as identified by the library staff through May 29, 1982. Funding for the major portion of the preparation of the *Serials List* was obtained through two HEA Title II-C grants from the U.S. Department of Education. Three indexes, *Title Index, Country of Publication Index,* and the *Mexican American Serials Index,* are provided to give access to the material in the Serials List in ways considered appropriate to the special nature of the Benson Collection holdings.

Alfred Cortot Collection. Eighty 16th through 18th century psalters and other liturgical music collected by the late French musician (1877–1962).

Medici Collection. Four hundred 16th and 17th century Florentine and Tuscan books pertaining to the Medici family and Florence.

Carl H. Pforzheimer Library of English Literature, 1475–1700. Until the library acquired it, this was the last major privately held collection of works representing the foundations of English culture. The collection includes the first book printed in the English language—Raoul Le Fevre's *Recuyell of the historyes of Troye* (1475). (The word Recuyell refers to an anthology.) Also included among the rare masterworks are the poetry, prose, and drama of Chaucer, Spenser, Shakespeare, Bacon, Donne, Milton, and other eminent literary figures from the 15th–17th centuries, as well as the first printed translations in English of several classical and continental writers such as Aristotle, St. Augustine, and Cervantes. The Pforzheimer Library is composed of more than 1,100 volumes and about 250 manuscript groups of letters and documents spanning some 225 years.

Among notable items in the library are: The four Shakespeare folios, dated 1623, 1632, 1663, and 1685. Spenser's *The Faerie Queen* (1590). Thomas Hooker's *Of the Lawes of Ecclesiasticall Politie,* printed between 1594 and 1597, considered the first statement of the principles behind the constitution of England, and Capt. John Smith's *The Generall Historie of Virginia* (1624), the first sizable work written in English about the new-found continent of North America.

The Uzielli Collection. A prize collection of 287 classical texts printed between 1495 and 1588 in Venice under the imprint of the noted Aldine Press contains the most famous of all Aldine editions—a five-volume set of Aristotle's works, 1495–1498, the first major Greek text to be reintroduced in the original to the Western world by the invention of the printing press. Other volumes include *Erotemata* (1495) by Constantine Lascaris, *Hypnerotomachia Poliphili* (1499) by Francesco Colonna, a 1501 edition of Virgil's writings, and two volumes of Plato (1513) printed on vellum, the first edition of Plato in the original Greek.

W. E. van Wijk Chronology Collection. Fifteen hundred 15th through 20th century European works on chronology, calendars, almanacs, and astronomy.

Other notable collections cataloged on OCLC for the Humanities Research Center, University of Texas at Austin, include the personal libraries of:

W.H. Auden and Chester Kallman (400 titles); James Joyce (550 titles from his residences in Trieste and Zurich, 1905–1920); Compton Mackenzie (7,500 titles); Christopher Morley (6,000 titles); Ezra Pound (635 titles); Anne Sexton (750 titles); Edith Sitwell (300 titles); and Gloria Swanson (100 titles)

The University of Texas at El Paso (TXU)
El Paso, TX

The Chicano Collection. This 1,500-volume collection contains mostly books and audiovisual materials on Mexican Americans.

The Carl Hertzog Collection. This 2,000-volume collection includes all of the titles published by Dr. Hertzog, as well as books about books and book people, and books on typography, design, and the history of printing.

The Judaica Collection. This 1,100-volume collection concerns all phases of Jewish life and thought, especially religion, philosophy, literature, and law.

The S.L.A. Marshall Military Collection. This 5,700-volume collection contains all of General S.L.A. Marshall's published works, in addition to books on military history from ancient to modern times. It is strongest in the United States' involvement in the wars of the 20th century.

The Southwest Collection. This 9,000-volume collection consists of books on the history and literature of the city of El Paso; the states of Texas, New Mexico, and Arizona; and northern Mexico.

The Western Fiction Collection. This 1,500-volume collection contains a comprehensive selection of Western American fiction from its 19th century beginnings to contemporary authors.

The University of Utah (UUM)
Salt Lake City, UT

Afro-American Rare Book Collection. Consists of 160 titles in microfiche. The collection was selected from the holdings of the Western States Black Research Center in Los Angeles. The items contained in the collection are mostly books, usually first edi-

August 18, 1932

Dear Mrs. Wesenberg: Of course, I remember
my visit to Indianapolis and everything concern-
in it — especially the Wesenbergs. How
could I possibly forget the city that boasts
the author of "Sapphire Nights" as a respectable
tax-payer!

I need not add that your appreciation of "The
Book of Living Verse" is particularly
gratifying. You may be interested to know
that an English edition is impending and
that a rather swank edition is going to be
set up on the Continent and one of its
foremost printers is going to do it. I think

I think your term "vowel slides " describing
Emily Dickinson's phonetic shifts is particularly
apt and I hope you will send me a copy of the
article when it appears. I happen to have
collected E. D. data for the last six or seven
years and, having rather specialized on the
topic, I feel a book on E. D., her legend,
her temperament and her technic, will be
my labor for 1935.

With kindest remembrances to your husband,
I am,

Cordially yours,

Louis Untermeyer .

tions, many of unique or of limited printings, which were written primarily in the 19th and early 20th centuries.

Landmarks of Science Collection. Landmarks of Science and Landmarks II constitute two comprehensive collections of materials relating to the history of science. The first Landmarks program was begun by the Readex Microprint Corporation in 1967 and is primarily based on the history of science collections housed at the University of Oklahoma and the British Museum. Scientific monographs dating from the beginning of printing comprise the first set. About 3,460 titles are included in this set. Landmarks II is an ongoing project to add significant works to the collection, particularly journals which became a major method of communication among scientists after 1650.

College of William and Mary (VWL)
Williamsburg, VA

Armistead Collection. Includes 243 volumes representing 94 titles and consists of the predominant legal materials of a practicing lawyer in 19th century Virginia. The books were assembled by the Armistead family during their many years of residence in Williamsburg. The collection was given by the family in memory of Robert Henry Armistead, a College of William and Mary graduate who received his degree in 1832.

Jefferson Collection. The Jefferson Collection is being reconstructed from the *Catalogue of the Library of Thomas Jefferson* by E. Millicent Sowerby, (Library of Congress, 1952). This collection, consisting of 130 volumes representing 85 titles, will replicate the law library offered to Congress by Thomas Jefferson after the original Library of Congress was destroyed during the War of 1812. The collection is expected to grow to approximately 450 titles.

Roman Law Collection. This collection consists of 326 volumes representing 216 titles and includes all English-language texts on the subject published from the mid-19th century to date.

Eastern Mennonite College (VEM)
Harrisonburg, VA

Menno Simons Historical Library/Archives. A collection of approximately 16,300 volumes (of which approximately 20% have been cataloged on OCLC) relative to Anabaptist and Mennonite history, doctrine, sociology, genealogy, and the arts, including imprints from the 16th century to the present. An additional focus is on regional history, especially the German element in the Shenandoah Valley, its history, music, genealogy, and publishing.

University of Richmond (VRU)
Richmond, VA

Meredith Collection of Confederate Imprints. This collection of approximately 500 imprints includes official publications of the Confederate government, as well as nonofficial publications. Most of the official documents were printed in the Confederate capital, Richmond, but many others were printed by army units in the field or by printers in other southern states. The nonofficial publication holdings input include military manuals, biography and history, description and travel, political and other pamphlets, maps, music scores, playbills, broadsides, texts, religious materials, and varieties of belles lettres representing "the various types of publications necessary for day-to-day existence [in] a 19th century nation."

University of Virginia (VA@)
Charlottesville, VA

African History Collection. Approximately 7,000 titles in the "DT" class have been processed through OCLC or were converted in a special project in 1982. With the exception of Arabic materials and a few other items in non-Roman alphabets, these works represent the entire DT portion of the University of Virginia's collections, including rare books. A locally-produced microfiche listing of these materials was produced from the machine-readable records. It consists of a dictionary catalog of authors, titles, and subjects and a list of call number order. Each access point contains an abbreviated record.

Clifton Waller Barrett Library of American Literature Collection. The bulk of the Barrett collection of 250,000 books and manuscripts contains fiction, poetry, drama, essays, and letters of American authors, and its approximately 50,000 volumes are a very nearly complete collection of the publications of every major American literary author up to 1950. The 5,000 titles thus far converted through OCLC are the Barrett/Wright collection of Minor American Novels based on Lyle H. Wright's *American Fiction, 1774–1900* and a similar collection of minor American poetry based on Oscar Wagelin's *Early American Poetry.* The collection is continuing to grow and new acquisitions are routinely cataloged through OCLC.

Tracy W. McGregor Library of American History Collection. The collection consists of important works related to American history, beginning with the early voyages of discovery and exploration, with a particular emphasis on what is now the southeastern United States. Approximately 2,700 titles from the 18th century portion of the collection have been converted; work on the remaining 14,000 titles began in 1984 with Title II-C funding. Current acquisitions are cataloged through OCLC routinely.

Polish Collection. Approximately 6,500 titles of works written in Polish or about Poland have been processed through OCLC or converted in a special project. A microfiche catalog was produced from the machine-readable records. It consists of author-title, subject, and call number sections, with full records for main entries in the shelflist portion and brief records at other access points.

Sadleir-Black Collection of Gothic Novels. Consists of 1,171 titles of Gothic fiction of the late 18th and the 19th centuries.

University of Virginia School of Law (VAL)
Charlottesville, VA

Newlin Collection on Oceans Law and Policy. Approximately 6,300 monographic and serial titles—hardcopy, microform, maps, charts, videotape, and sound recordings—on maritime law and policy materials. The collection is supplemented by extensive holdings of supporting general and technical research works. Also well represented are documents from all levels of government, local to international.

University of Washington Libraries (WAU)
Seattle, WA

Forest Resources Collection. The Forest Resources Collection includes approximately 23,000 titles located primarily in the Forest Resources Library. The collection is international in scope and is composed of books and serials on all forestry-related subjects, including forest biology and ecology, forest products, wood technology and utilization, pulp and paper technology, and utilization of forested lands, including conservation and outdoor recreation. A list of titles added before 1981 is available on microfiche from the libraries' Publications Office.

Pacific Northwest Newspapers Collection. The University of Washington Libraries has added to the OCLC database records for 425 newspapers of historical significance in the Pacific Northwest, some of which are unique to this collection.

The State Historical Society of Wisconsin (WIH)
Madison, WI

U.S. Army Military History Research Collection of Camp Newspapers. This collection of approximately 2,000 newspapers from all the services was assembled and microfilmed in 1972 at the U.S. Army War College Library, Carlisle Barracks, Pa. Over 300 titles have been entered in OCLC. The State Historical Society has also cataloged numerous other unnamed collections on OCLC. Among them are Wisconsin state government publications, trade union publications, a large pamphlet collection, and various periodical collections (alternative press, genealogical, Native American, and women's).

University of Wisconsin—Madison (GZM)
Madison, WI

William B. Cairns Collection. This collection of the works of American women writers before 1900 has several parts. In a section of significant authors (Alcott, Bradstreet, Chopin, Dickinson, Freeman, Gilman, Jewett, Fuller, and Stowe) the library collects all variants of all works, including some manuscript material. For other writers, of whom there are currently over 300, the library collects at least one copy of each title published. A reference collection of bibliographies and critical works aids access to the collection. The collection includes fiction, poetry, science fiction, diaries, and travel accounts.

William A. Cole Collection. Purchased in 1977, this collection of books on the history of chemistry contains approximately 675 titles. The collection contains three 16th century works and a large number of 17th and 18th century titles, many of which are quite scarce. Such notable scientists as Lavoisier, Lemery, and Priestley are well represented in the collection in first and other editions.

Twentieth Century Collection. Established in the late 1960s, this collection includes first and other important editions of the works of more than 200 significant British and American authors. The list of authors includes both the "greats" of the early 20th century and a number of contemporary writers whose works have lasting merit.

George White Collection. The approximately 280 titles on the history of geology place this collection among the top three in the country in holdings of early geologic literature. The collection is especially strong in English and French books of the 18th and 19th centuries and in the history of glaciology.

University of Wisconsin—Milwaukee (GZN)
Milwaukee, WI

Roman Ecclesiastical Architecture Collection. This collection of approximately 400 titles includes books dating from the 16th–20th centuries and primarily concerned with Roman ecclesiastical architecture between A.D. 313 and around 1400. Most of the publications are illustrated and range from pamphlets to multivolume sets. The texts are in Latin, Italian, German, French, and English. The approach is broadly historical and civic architecture is also represented, as are some sites closely allied to Rome.

University of Newcastle-upon-Tyne (EUN)
Newcastle-upon-Tyne, United Kingdom

Pybus Collection. The collection was built by the late Professor F.C. Pybus, professor of surgery at the university, over a period of 40 years and comprises 2,500 volumes, 2,000 engravings, 50 portraits and busts, and a large number of holograph letters. The books are classics of the history of medicine, with particular reference to the history of anatomy, of surgery, and of medical illustrations. The engravings, oil paintings, and busts are of medical men from the 16th to the 20th century. The book catalog for this collection is OCLC #8246526.

TAB. IV.

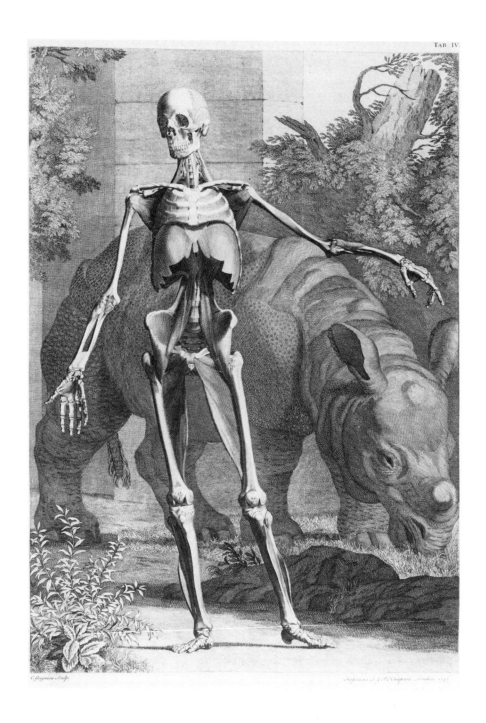

Medical illustration by the German anatomist Bernard Siegfried Albinus (1697–1770) from the Pybus Collection, University Library, University of Newcastle-upon-Tyne. The drawing is from his Tabulaesceleti et Musculorum Corporis Humani (1749).

Appendix A: Languages in the Database

Acholi
Afrihili
Afrikaans
Afro-Asiatic
Akkadian
Albanian
Aleut
Algonquian
  languages
Aljamia
Amharic
Anglo-Saxon
Apache
Arabic
Aramaic
Arapaho
Araucanian
Arawak
Armenian
Assamese
Athapascan
  languages
Avaric
Avesta
Awadhi
Aymara
Azerbaijani
Baltic
Baluchi
Bambara
Bashkir
Basque
Beja
Belorussian
Bemba
Bengali
Berber languages
Bhojpuri
Blackfoot
Braj
Breton
Bulgarian
Burmese
Caddo
Cambodian
Carib
Catalan
Caucasian
Central American
  Indian
Chechen
Cherokee
Cheyenne
Chibcha
Chinese
Chinook
Choctaw
Church Slavic
Chuvash
Coptic
Cornish
Cree
Creoles and
  Pidgins

Cushitic
Czech
Dakota
Danish
Delaware
Dinka
Dogri
Dravidian
Duala
Dutch
Dutch, Middle
  (ca. 1050–1350)
Efik
Egyptian
Elamite
English
English, Middle
  (ca. 1100–1500)
Eskimo
Esperanto
Estonian
Ethiopic
Ewe
Fang
Faroese
Finnish
Fon
French
French, Middle
  (ca. 1500–1700)
French, Old
  (ca. 842–1500)
Frisian
Ga
Gaelic (Scots)
Galla
Georgian
German
German, Middle
  High (ca. 1050–
  1500)
German, Old High
  (ca. 750–1050)
Germanic (Other)
Gondi
Gothic
Greek, Ancient
  (to 1453)
Greek, Modern
Guarani
Gujarati
Haida
Hausa
Hawaiian
Hebrew
Herero
Himachali
Hindi
Hungarian
Hupa
Icelandic
Ilocano
Indic
Indo-European

Indonesian
Interlingua
Iranian
Irish
Iroquoian
  languages
Italian
Japanese
Javanese
Judeo-Arabic
Judeo-Persian
Kachin
Kamba
Kannada
Kanuri
Karakalpak
Karen
Kashmiri
Kazakh
Khotanese
Kikuyu
Kinyarwanda
Kirghiz
Kongo
Konkani
Korean
Kpelle
Kru
Kurdish
Kurukh
Kutenai
Ladino
Lahnda
Lamba
Lao
Lapp
Latin
Latvian
Lithuanian
Lolo (Bantu)
Luba
Luganda
Luiseno
Macedonian
Magahi
Maithili
Malagasy
Malay
Malayalam
Malayo-Polynesian
Maltese
Mandingo
Manobo
Maori
Marathi
Marwari
Masai
Mayan languages
Mende
Micmac
Mohawk
Moldavian

Mongol
Mossi
Muskogee
Nahuatlan
Navajo
Nepali
Newari
Niger-Congo
North American
  Indian
Northern Sotho
Norwegian
Nubian
Nyamwezi
Nyanja
Nyoro
Ojibwa
Oriya
Osage
Ossetic
Otomian
  languages
Ottoman Turkish
Pahlavi
Pali
Panjabi
Papuan-Australian
Persian, Modern
Persian, Old
  (ca. 600–
  400 B.C.)
Polish
Portuguese
Prakrit
Provencal
Pushto
Quechua
Rajasthani
Rhaeto-Romance
Romance
Romanian
Romany
Rundi
Russian
Salishan languages
Samaritan Aramaic
Sandawe
Sango
Sanskrit
Selkup
Semitic
Serbo-Croatian
  (Cyrillic)
Serbo-Croatian
  (Roman)
Serer
Shan
Shona
Sidamo
Sindhi
Sinhalese
Sino-Tibetan
Siouan languages
Slavic

Slovak
Slovenian
Sogdian
Somali
Songhai
South American
  Indian
Southern Sotho
Spanish
Sub-Saharan
  African
Sukuma
Sumerian
Susu
Swahili
Swedish
Syriac
Tagalog
Tajik
Tamil
Tatar
Telugu
Temne
Tereno
Thai
Tibetan
Tigre
Tigrina
Tlingit
Tsimshian
Tswana
Turkish
Turkmen
Turko-Tataric
Twi
Ugaritic
Uigur
Ukrainian
Umbundu
Urdu
Uzbek
Vietnamese
Votic
Wakashan
  languages
Walamo
Walsho
Welsh
Wendic
Wolof
Xhosa
Yao (Bantu)
Yiddish
Yoruba
Zapotec
Zenaga
Zulu
Zuni

Appendix B: Title II-C Projects

The "Strengthening Research Library Resources Program" of the Higher Education Act, Title II-C, provided $5.74 million for 38 projects in fiscal year (FY) 1986. The funds support bibliographic control ($4.42 million), preservation ($1.12 million), and collection development ($190,217). Nineteen of the projects will result in significant additions of bibliographic records and holdings information to the OCLC Online Union Catalog. Project grants involving the OCLC database accounted for $3.14 million.

The U.S. Department of Education received 97 proposals; a total of $18.75 million in program funds was requested for FY 1986.

The following abstracts are based on *Library Programs, HEA Title II-C, Abstracts of Funded Projects, 1986,* published by the U.S. Department of Education.

American Museum of Natural History: To microfilm, restore, and conserve some 80 unique scientific and historic ledgers, scrapbooks, field diaries and notebooks, and specimen catalogs from scientific expeditions, fieldwork, and laboratory work, which form a unique record of the development of science and a major scientific institution in the United States.

Dartmouth College: To improve accessibility and availability of the Dartmouth College Library collections in theatre and the performing arts, a comprehensive resource consisting of monographs, periodicals, newspapers, scripts, libretti, programs, playbills, scrapbooks, slides, sheet music, and other materials providing primary source materials for research in the performing arts.

Duke University: To convert the current serials holdings of Duke University, North Carolina State University at Raleigh, and University of North Carolina at Chapel Hill to machine-readable form.

Emory University: To conduct a retrospective conversion, cataloging, and preservation project for a discrete collection of 16,977 titles of 18th-century imprints in the subject areas of philosophy and religion.

Houston Academy of Medicine-Texas Medical Center: To catalog a comprehensive special collection—the Burbank-Fraser Collection on Arthritis, Rheumatism, and Gout, enter the data into the OCLC network, provide the cataloging worksheets to the University of Pittsburgh's Falk Library, and publicize the collection to historians, researchers, and libraries.

Massachusetts Institute of Technology: To provide national access to the Massachusetts Institute of Technology Libraries' collection of scientific and technological publications issued by the Institute from 1861 through 1974 by cataloging and adding full MARC records to OCLC.

Missouri Botanical Garden: To increase the accessibility for the nation's research and academic library community to the extensive collections of plant science literature held in the libraries of the Missouri Botanical Garden and The New York Botanical Garden, the nation's two most comprehensive botanical libraries.

The Ohio State University: To preserve and provide online bibliographic access to the unique collection of medieval and medieval tradition (13th through 20th century) Slavic Cyrillic manuscripts in microform in the Hilander Research Library.

State Historical Society of Wisconsin: To make the "Cutter Pamphlets," a general collection of unbound ephemera emphasizing social and cultural history collected from 1854 to 1966, more accessible to researchers across the nation by preserving materials needing basic conversion measures and by entering full MARC records into OCLC for all items not now in the database.

University of California, Berkeley: To make research materials in the Bancroft Library more available to scholars by converting 50,000 card catalog records for printed materials into machine-readable form.

University of California, San Diego: To strengthen the Archive for New Poetry through a collection-building effort that will ensure comprehensive coverage for 50 poets and extend access to the materials to the international scholarly community through cataloging, preservation, and dissemination of information.

University of Illinois: To conduct a retrospective cataloging and indexing program to strengthen the research collections of the University of Illinois Agriculture Library and to improve national and international access to hardcopy sets of United States Department of Agriculture and state experiment station agricultural materials, dating from 1862 to the present, through series analytics on the OCLC database and indexing on the AGRICOLA and AGRIS databases.

University of Kansas: To continue the cataloging of serials and ephemeral materials contained in the Wilcox Collection of Contemporary Political Movements, an outstanding special collection of American extremist political literature.

University of Kentucky: To continue efforts to preserve and make bibliographically available the University of Kentucky's extensive Kentuckiana Collection of maps, broadsides, manuscripts, correspondence, and other archival resources.

University of Maryland College Park: To provide machine-readable cataloging records over a two-year period for Segment 2 of the microfilm collection *Goldsmiths'-Kress Library of Economic Literature,* which consists of 29,412 titles on 1,669 reels.

University of Minnesota: To improve scholarly access to the University of Minnesota's extensive Scandinavian holdings.

University of Missouri-Columbia: To provide or improve bibliographic access to approximately 10,710 pre-1800 imprints held by the University of Missouri-Columbia Libraries by providing full cataloging for these scarce, valuable, or unique titles and entering the records into the OCLC database.

University of Pittsburgh: To provide nationwide access to the unique John A. Nietz Textbook Collection, one of the three largest pre-1900 American textbook collections in the United States.

University of Wisconsin-Madison: To create and add machine-readable records of the outstanding collection of 25,000 pieces of musical theater performance materials known as the Tams-Witmark Collection to the OCLC and RLIN databases; clean, preserve, and store the physical documents; and make films available on demand to the scholarly and performing communities.

Appendix C: Major Microforms Projects

Sets in Progress (No Release Dates Available)

Title of Set (Set Symbol)	Institution (OCLC Symbol)	Approx. Titles
American Medical Periodicals, 1797–1900 (AMV)	University of Wisconsin-Madison, Health Sciences Library (GZH)	2,600
American Poetry II (POF)	University of Georgia (GUA)	3,000
American Poetry III (POG)	University of Georgia (GUA)	6,000
Black Culture Collection (BHZ)	Central State University (CNC)	150
British Naval History Collection	U.S. Naval War College (WNC)	217
Canon Law (LCW)	St. Louis University Law Library (SLU)	
Civil Law (CVW)	St. Louis University Law Library (SLU)	
The Cox Library (CWX)	Smithsonian Institute Libraries/ OCLC RETROCON	
Early English Books (Units 1–32) (EAA)	Indiana University (IUL)	25,000
Gerritsen Collection of Women's History (WZZ)	University Microfilms International (UMI)	4500
Goldsmiths'-Kress Library of Economic Literature (GKR)	University of Maryland (UMC)	30,000
History of Photography (FOT)	Smithsonian Institute Libraries/ OCLC RETROCON	2,200
Inter-University Consortium for Political & Social Research (PSX)	University of Utah (UUM)	1,500
Library of English Literature (LEL)	College of Charleston (SBM)	2500
LC, Jakarta Office, Southeast Asia Microfiche, 1981–85 (AYT)	Ohio University (OUN)	3,500
Manuscripta (MMZ)	Southern Methodist University (SMU)	1,300
Pamphlets of American History Collection (Unit 1) (PMZ)	Smithsonian Institute Libraries/ OCLC RETROCON	5,300
Stafleu & Cowan/Taxonomic Literature (TLZ)	Missouri Botanical Garden Library (MOA)	5,000
Yale Law Library Blackstone Collection (BLY)	Mississippi College Law Library (MCC)	280

Sets Available

Title of Set (Set Symbol)	Institution (OCLC Symbol)	No. of Titles
Adelaide Nutting Historical Nursing Collection	University Microfilms International (UMI)	1,204
‡American Autobiographies	OCLC RETROCON®	450
‡American Culture Series I	OCLC RETROCON	2,000
American Periodicals I (PER)	New York State Library (NYG)	105
American Periodicals II (PES)	New York State Library (NYG)	1,409
American Periodicals III (PEA)	New York State Library (NYG)	212
American Poetry I (POE)	University of Georgia (GUA)	2,000
*American Political Science Association Proceedings, 1982 (PRO)	University of Calif., Inst. of Governmental Studies (CBG)	1,200
*American Theological Library Association Preservation Records	American Theological Library (ATL)	4,000
British & Continental Rhetoric and Elocution (BRT)	Mansfield University (MAN)	116
Crime & Juvenile Delinquency, 1981, 1984–85, 1985–1986, 1987	University Microfilms International (UMI)	1,429
Dime Novels (Units 1–7)	University Microfilms International (UMI)	3,104
Early American Medical Imprints (EAM)	University of Calif., Davis, Health Sciences (CUX)	1,700
Early American Imprints: Second Series (Shaw-Shoemaker Series) (STF)	Stanford University (STF)	37,841
*Early English Books (Units 33–59) (Wing)	University Microfilms International (UMI)	15,583
Early English Newspapers (Units 1–42) (NEZ)	Purdue University (IPL)	920
Energy & Agriculture, Base Collection, 1984	University Microfilms International (UMI)	2,103
English & American Plays of the 19th Century (EAD)	Indiana University (IUL)	10,937
Food & Nutrition, 1983	University Microfilms International (UMI)	597
*Genealogy & Local History (Units 1–13)	University Microfilms International (UMI)	7,104
Health Care, 1980	University Microfilms International (UMI)	239
*Health, Physical Education and Recreation Microform Publications, 1985, 1986, 1987	SUNY College at Brockport (XBM)	1,685
‡History of Women, Research Publications	OCLC RETROCON	7,000
Housing & Urban Affairs 1977, 1979, 1980	University Microfilms International (UMI)	650
‡Human Relations Area File	OCLC RETROCON	2,300

*International Law (Unit 1–3) (LWK)	St. Louis University Law Library (SLU)	1,017
Jewish Theological Seminary: Adler	University Microfilms International (UMI)	355
Jewish Theological Seminary: History of Science	University Microfilms International (UMI)	405
Jewish Theological Seminary: Maimonides	University Microfilms International (UMI)	71
Landmarks of Science I (UGR)	University of Utah (UUM)	3,812
Landmarks of Science II (UGT)	University of Utah (UUM)	5,430
LC, Jakarta Office, Southeast Asia Microfiche, 1978–80 Collection (AYS)	Ohio University (OUN)	3,187
Library of American Civilization (ACV)	Mankato State University (MNM)	12,000
Lyle H. Wright's American Fiction (LWS)	University of Arizona (AZU)	9,450
Model Cities	University Microfilms International (UMI)	869
National Resources Planning Board Reports	University Microfilms International (UMI)	199
19th-Century British Books and Pamphlets on Microfiche	Chadwick-Healey Limited (CDY)	200,000
*19th Century Legal Treatise (Units 1–21) (NLT)	St. Louis University Law Library (SLU)	4,781
Pamphlets in American History Collection (Units 2–5)	University Microfilms International (UMI)	12,285
*Pre-1900 Canadiana (Units 1–21)	University Microfilms International (UMI)	41,415
Presidential Election Campaign Biographies 1824–1976	University Microfilms International (UMI)	465
Rehabilitation and Handicapped Literature, 1980, 1981, 1982–85	University Microfilms International (UMI)	881
*Russian History and Culture (Units 1–20)	University Microfilms International (UMI)	2,128
‡Selected Americana from Sabin	OCLC RETROCON	11,000
‡Slavery Source Materials	OCLC RETROCON	450
Source Materials in the Field of Theater (THE)	Mansfield University (MAN)	76
Spanish Civil War Collection (SWZ)	University of California, San Diego (CUS)	2,226
Spanish Drama of the Golden Age (SPG)	University of Missouri (MUU)	411
Three Centuries of English & American Plays (TCR)	Indiana University (IUL)	4,090
‡Underground Press Collection	OCLC RETROCON	900
Utopian Literature	University Microfilms International (UMI)	461
‡Western Americana	OCLC RETROCON	6,000

* Other units forthcoming
‡ Records derived from OCLC RETROCON projects

Appendix D: OCLC Online Union Catalog

The OCLC Online Union Catalog is a database of bibliographic information. Each record in the Online Union Catalog contains the bibliographic description of a single work and each record is assigned a unique control number (its OCLC number). With this computerized database, only one library prepares the original catalog entry for an item. Each participating library contributes to the Online Union Catalog a record for an item not already cataloged by another library. A library enters a record directly into the Online Union Catalog through a series of online transactions, basically filling out an blank electronic "form."

Other libraries search this online catalog using the search "keys" to find a record describing the item they wish to catalog. Once the record is found (94% of the time), a library can "temporarily modify" it to conform to local needs and standards for the automatic production of conventional catalog cards, accessions lists of newly cataloged materials, and magnetic tapes of these machine-readable records.

In addition to bibliographic information, the Online Union Catalog contains location information. With each record is a list of symbols that identify participating libraries that have used that record for cataloging. As a result, subsequent cataloging, acquisitions, interlibrary loan, and serials control processes are streamlined. The OCLC-Library of Congress Name-Authority File is also readily available online for verifying the form of cataloging entries.

Other online files contain administrative information (addresses, lending policies, etc.) about OCLC members, vendors, and other agencies (publishers, et al.). Users retrieve this information in seconds by typing simple commands on their terminal keyboard.

Index

A

B

C

OCLC Online Computer Library Center, a nonprofit membership organization, is engaged in computer library service and research and makes available computer-based processes, products and services for libraries and other educational organizations, and library users. From its facility in Dublin, Ohio, OCLC operates an international computer network that libraries use to acquire and catalog books, order custom-printed catalog cards and machine-readable records for local catalogs, arrange interlibrary loans, maintain location information on library materials, and gain access to other databases. OCLC also provides local decentralized computer systems and stand-alone microcomputer-based systems for individual libraries or clusters of libraries, and online and offline products and services for the electronic delivery of information.

More than 8,000 libraries contribute to and/or use information in the OCLC Online Union Catalog, the world's largest database of library bibliographic information. OCLC has participating libraries in the following countries: Australia, Barbados, Belgium, Canada, People's Republic of China, Costa Rica, Denmark, Federal Republic of Germany, Finland, France, Iceland, Ireland, Italy, Japan, Mexico, Netherlands, Oman, Puerto Rico, Saudi Arabia, Spain, Sweden, Switzerland, Taiwan, United Kingdom, United States, and Vatican City.

Reader Comments

In addition to information regarding your special collections, OCLC looks forward to receiving your comments and suggestions concerning this publication. Indicate your opinion of how well the guide meets these objectives by checking the appropriate box:

	STRONGLY AGREE	AGREE	NO OPINION	DISAGREE*	STRONGLY DISAGREE*
Guide is easy to read.	☐	☐	☐	☐	☐
Guide is well organized.	☐	☐	☐	☐	☐
Guide is at the right technical level.	☐	☐	☐	☐	☐
Index is at the right level of detail.	☐	☐	☐	☐	☐
Index is easy to use.	☐	☐	☐	☐	☐
Guide is attractive.	☐	☐	☐	☐	☐

Enter other comments below. Please note any errors (by page number when possible). If you need more space, use blank sheets or photocopies of pages from the Guide to record your comments and mail in an envelope to the address noted on the reverse side of this form.

Persons I will share this guide with:
Faculty ☐ Administrators ☐ Library staff ☐ Patrons ☐ Other: _____

OPTIONAL

Name	Date
Address	

Fold and tape.
Do not staple.

BUSINESS REPLY MAIL

FIRST CLASS   PERMIT NO. 11   DUBLIN, OHIO

POSTAGE WILL BE PAID BY ADDRESSEE

OCLC
Special Collections Guide, MC 123
6565 Frantz Road
Dublin, Ohio 43017-9983